SPEAK FOR YOURSELF!

Phototypeset from author's disk by Piccadilly Press.
Printed and bound by Redwood Books, Trowbridge,
for the publishers Piccadilly Press Ltd.,
5 Castle Road, London NW1 8PR

A catalogue record for this book is available from the
British Library

ISBN: 1 85340 394 6 (hardback)
 1 85340 399 7 (trade paperback)

Rosie Rushton lives in Northamptonshire. She is a freelance
journalist with a special interest in teenage and relationship
issues and has a weekly column in *The Times*. Other books
she has written for Piccadilly Press include: YOU'RE MY BEST
FRIEND – I HATE YOU; STAYING COOL, SURVIVING SCHOOL; JUST
DON'T MAKE A SCENE, MUM; I THINK I'LL JUST CURL UP AND
DIE; HOW COULD YOU DO THIS TO ME, MUM? and most
recently, POPPY.

Cover design: Rebecca Elgar
Inside design: Sue Lambell

SPEAK FOR YOURSELF!

FINDING YOU VOICE AMONG YOUR PEERS

ROSIE RUSHTON

Piccadilly Press • London

CONTENTS

Chapter 5
SAYING NO

Chapter 6
OUT WITH IT: saying what you mean and meaning what you say

Chapter 7
FRIEND SPEAK

Chapter 8
PROBLEM FRIENDSHIP:
when bosom buddiness turns into mate hate

Chapter 9
PARENT SPEAK

THE FINAL WORD

INTRODUCTION

This book is about finding your voice. It won't help if you are looking for a herbal remedy for laryngitis or exquisitely difficult singing exercises designed to get you the lead at Covent Garden. What it will help you do is find ways round all those agonising moments when you have all the feelings – and no words to express them; when you have to say, "No", but, "Oh, all right then," seems much easier. It tries to sort out the differences between what you say and what you really mean, to find remedies for those times when you feel so shy that you are quite happy for everyone else to do the talking – and then find yourself doing things you never wanted to. It helps you find ways to make friends – and tactful ways to get them off your back!

It hasn't been written in order to tell you what to think or how to behave. It has been written because who you are and what you have to say matters.

So let's talk!

Chapter 1

• •

SHYNESS IS NOT JUST ABOUT SAYING HELLO

*"It's all right to have butterflies in your stomach.
Just get them to fly in formation."*
Dr Rob Gilbert, media doctor

When you are feeling shy, it seems as if everyone else in the world is brimming over with self-confidence. It's easy to imagine that no one else in the world gets tongue-tied, or blushes scarlet or utters a silent prayer that the ground will open and swallow them up. And the more you think that everyone else is a whiz-kid on the social scene, the more you believe that there is something wrong with you. It is true that there are some people who can walk into a room full of strangers, smile broadly and launch into a witty account of how they tackled the black run at Zermatt. They appear not to have a care in the world – but you will probably find they are terrified of spiders and faint at the sight of a needle. And you can be fairly certain that at least half of them are shy as well. The difference is that they have mastered the art of hiding it!

WHAT BEING SHY FEELS LIKE

Shyness is a miserable feeling. When you feel shy:

• You are convinced that you are a total nerd as well as being the ugliest and worst-dressed person in the room.
• You feel yourself blushing and you want the ground to open and swallow you up.
• You want everyone to look anywhere except at you because you are sure they are all noticing the spot on your chin or thinking your bottom looks fat in your new hipsters.
• You don't want anyone to speak to you because you are sure you won't know what to say back.
• You believe that it is your fault that you feel so awkward.
• You wish you had stayed at home with a good book.
• You swear you will never, ever get yourself into this situation again.

That's OK. It's allowed. Feeling shy is not a sin, and it is not your fault, any more than the shape of your nose or the size of your feet is your fault. And you would be surprised how many people suffer in just the same way.

Some people think that you are only shy if you blush easily. Certainly blushing is a sign of shyness but there are plenty of kids who never colour up but who suffer just as much. When shyness strikes, it can have all sorts of strange effects.

• Your tongue appears to be stuck to the roof of your mouth.
• Your stomach churns and you need to keep dashing to the loo.
• Your throat dries up and your voice goes squeaky.

- You turn bright red and feel hot.
- Your palms sweat and your hands shake.
- You feel sick.
- You can't bring yourself to look anyone in the eye.
- Your heart thunders as if you had just done the 1500m steeplechase.
- You feel like crying.

Not only does all this make you feel pretty awful, but it has other drawbacks too. Being shy makes it harder to make friends, stops you from speaking up for your rights and prevents you from voicing your opinions. It also makes it harder for other people to get the chance to discover how interesting you are, and makes you feel different from the rest of the gang, isolated and alone.

That is why it is worth trying to zap shyness on the head before it gets out of control.

WHAT MAKES YOU SHY?

Different people are shy for different reasons and in different situations and everybody feels shy sometimes.

There is much more to feeling shy than trembling when you are introduced to your girlfriend's mum or finding that your voice goes all squeaky when someone asks your name. Even if you can handle those first introductions without too much trouble, you may well feel shy when:

- You are with someone you really want to impress – like the girl of your dreams or your boyfriend's father

– and you are scared of making a fool of yourself.
• You have to strike up a conversation with someone new – and can't think of a thing to say.
• You really like someone and want to be their friend – but don't know how they feel about you.
• Someone asks your opinion – and you are sure they know more about it than you do.
• You are being asked to do something you don't want to do – and you are afraid that if you say no you will fall out with your friends.
• You have strong feelings and don't know how to express them – but know you need to talk.
• You are in a situation where you are the centre of attention – and you don't want to be!

Three ways in which teenagers overcame shyness

Bryony, Glenn and Stephanie all say that they are shy people. But when you ask them what they mean they give very different answers.

Bryony is 13.
"I don't mind going to parties and meeting new people; what really scares me is when I get to know them better and they start asking questions about me and my family. My dad is in prison for taking some money from the company he worked for. When I admitted that to someone at school her mum said she didn't want Lisa to come to our house any more because we were a bad lot. After that, I felt that everyone was looking down on me and I felt really isolated."

Glenn is 14 and has a stammer.
"I get really uptight about any situation where people expect

me to chat. When I have difficulty getting a word out, some guys get impatient and finish the sentence for me – and so often they assume what I want to say and get it wrong. Then I get flustered and the stammer gets worse. Sometimes I think it's easier to avoid getting involved in the first place."

Stephanie is 12 and was involved in a car accident when she was eight.
"I have quite a bit of facial scarring. My friends don't notice it any more, so I am fine when I am with them. But when I go shopping or eat in a restaurant some people turn and stare and then I feel myself going bright red and feel sick."

Bryony felt shy because of the way people reacted to her family circumstances, Glenn was embarrassed by his difficulty in speaking, and while Stephanie had no problem being outgoing with her own friends, she felt insecure when people she had never met took notice of her. But they found their own ways to zap that shyness.

"It was my uncle who helped me," said Bryony. *"He suggested that I should tell my friends that Dad had made a big mistake and paid for it, but that didn't make us bad or different from anyone else. It took a lot of doing, but I really found that people accepted what I said – and I felt really chuffed about having had the courage to say it!"*

Glenn was also brave. He told his closest mates how uncomfortable it made him feel to be continually interrupted and said that just because he had a stammer, it didn't mean that what he had to say was not important. *"When they began waiting to let me get the words out, I began finding it easier to speak,"* he said. *"If I hadn't admitted how I felt, things would just have got worse."*

Stephanie can now eat in a restaurant without feeling uncomfortable. *"My sister, who is 16, was brilliant. She told me to look people in the eye and give a big grin when I saw them staring at me. It was ages before I could do it, but when I did it worked! They either grinned back or else realised how rude they were being and stopped looking at me. Either way, I felt much better!"*

I CAN'T DO THAT – I'M SHY! – using it as an excuse

Sometimes it is even *comfortable* to be shy. Some people use their shyness as an excuse. They say things like:

"I'm a shy person – so I won't volunteer to help out on Parents Evening."

"I'm shy – so I needn't bother to make friendly conversation with my parents' friends."

"I'm a shy person – so I won't sign up to take part in the school concert."

"I'm shy, so I won't introduce myself to that new girl."

"I'm a shy person – so I won't accept that invitation in case I feel left out."

It's not that you actually address those words to yourself out loud. You have simply become so used to thinking of yourself as A Shy Person – in the way others see themselves (or you!) as An Artistic Person or An Athletic Person – that it never crosses your mind that you have the power to do something about it.

You probably think that what makes you feel shy is your fear of other people. You may feel fine talking to your friends, but panic about having a conversation with their parents. You may be happy talking to teachers but die of embarrassment if you need to tell a shop assistant that the sweater you bought has shrunk in the wash. It isn't really the *people* who scare you: the person you are most afraid of is you. You worry that you won't say the right thing or make the right impression and that as a result everyone will give up on you or make fun of you.

What you tell yourself: I'm too shy to have dinner with my boyfriend's parents.
What really worries you: They might talk about things I know nothing about, and I will end up looking stupid.
What you can do about it: Find out what turns them on, mug up a couple of things to say ("Damon Hill had bad luck in the Grand Prix, didn't he?" or, "Do tell me about your trek to Nepal!"), and sit back and bask in their admiration! You won't have to talk for ages!

What you tell yourself: I want a new hairstyle but I don't dare go to a posh salon.
What really bothers you: I never dare to say no when they suggest doing something I don't fancy.
What you can do about it: Take along a picture of the style you want and ask whether your hair is suitable. If they say no, simply say, "Thank you – I will leave it for now." If they say yes it back and watch the new you emerge!

What you tell yourself: I'm not going to Jake's birthday

bash because I'm shy at those kind of things.

What really scares you: Rumour has it they are all going ice skating and I've never tried it and I am bound to be a dork at it.

What you can do about it: Go along, admit to being a beginner, laugh at yourself when you fall over and realise that when the gang giggle, they are laughing with you and not at you.

The truth is that few people notice half the things about you that you imagine they are noting down in great detail! Most people are too wrapped up thinking about what they are going to do next, or worrying about the impression *they* are making, to worry about whether you are turning pink or stumbling over a word.

HOW DO YOU HANDLE SHYNESS?

Try this quiz to find out how you handle those feelings of shyness.

1 Your friend is having a pool party and you feel shy about being seen in your swimsuit. Do you:

a) pretend you have another engagement?

b) go, but sit around in your skirt and baggy sweater and don't go in the water?

c) borrow your mum's rather snazzy sarong that she brought back from Bali, and wear it knotted round your waist to hide the chubby bits?

d) don a huge T-shirt and swim in that?

2 You spend all your allowance on a slinky lemon

shift dress, and a few days later the seam has ripped. Do you:

a) get your mum to take it back to the shop – she's much braver at that sort of thing?

b) sew it up yourself, even though it shows, rather than make a fuss?

c) get as far as the counter and then chicken out and go home?

d) ask a friend to come with you, take a deep breath and say, "I bought this on Saturday and it is falling to pieces. I am sure you will agree that is not acceptable"?

3 Your dad wants you to sell raffle tickets at his golf club Open Day. This means going up and speaking to a lot of people you have never met before. Do you:

a) say, "Not in a million years," and refuse to discuss it?

b) agree to do it – but then hide in the loo and hope the rest of the sellers make enough money?

c) carry out your duties by shoving a book of tickets under each person's nose and muttering, "Raffle"?

d) Take a deep breath, smile and say, "Excuse me, I am sure you would like the chance to win a day at the races – it's 20p a ticket"?

4 The gorgeous guy from next door, who has ignored your existence for years, suddenly asks you if you fancy a go on his rollerblades. You really fancy this guy – but you are terrified of falling over and looking a fool. Do you:

a) say, "No thanks," and look at your feet?

b) say, "I would, only you see I've got a bad foot – what happened was..." and launch into an elaborate – and fabricated – medical history?

c) say, "I'd rather sit here and watch the expert"?

d) say, "I'll try anything once if you don't mind picking up the pieces," take a deep breath and have a go?

Answers:

1 a) 0. For one thing, you will miss all the fun and for another, it will be twice as hard the next time a good invitation comes along.

b) 2. You're there, which means you can meet people and provided you look as if you are having a good time, no one is going to force you to strip off.

c) 4. Brilliant idea – you look really cool and everyone chats to you – if only to find out where they can get one!

d) 4. Another great idea – swim on your terms!

2 a) 2. If she offers, that's great – but go with her and pick up a few tips in shopper assertiveness.

b) 0. The fault lies with the manufacturer and once you try to bodge it up, the shop won't take it back – and you will be the loser.

c) 2. Two points for trying – but just think: what could happen? Not too many shoppers disappear without trace in John Lewis!

d) 4. Spot on. Being with a friend will help to boost your confidence (you can even practise what you are going to say in the Ladies beforehand!) and by saying "I am sure you will agree..." you are inviting the shop assistant to co-operate with you. Much better than, "You sold me this dud dress!"

3 a) 0. Not very helpful. If you are going to say no, at least give your father a reason.

b) 1. At least you made a gesture of helpfulness but you won't raise a lot of money in the loo and are letting the charity down.

c) 2. So-so. You will sell some tickets – but oh boy, will you be miserable doing it!

d) 4. Great all round. The guests will respond to your smile and invitation and probably spend twice as much as they intended to, you will feel fulfilled and each time you do it, it will get a little easier. And you never know just who might buy your next ticket!

4 a) 0. He made the effort to be friendly; the least you can do is afford him the same courtesy.

b) 1. If you can launch into an explanation as lengthy as that, you can tell the truth!

c) 3. That's a clever way of declining the offer but making the guy feel important and not sorry he spoke.

d) 5. Good. Humour is always an excellent way of handling shyness. A laugh is the best icebreaker known to the human race.

So how did you do?

0-6. You run the risk of missing out on a lot of the fun things in life, just through your insistence on playing safe. Set yourself the target of saying yes to one new thing each week – by the end of the month you will wonder what all the fuss was about.

6-14. You really do try to overcome your hang-ups. Occasionally the terror gets the better of you, but don't let that put you off. Just try again next time.

Over 14. You are already well on the road to overcoming shyness. You have discovered that, hard though those first words may be, it really is worth the effort.

Chapter 2
• •

SO JUST WHO DO YOU THINK YOU ARE?

"We forfeit three-fourths of ourselves to be like other people."
Arthur Schopenhauer, German philosopher (1788-1860)

Before you can begin to feel comfortable with other people, you have to feel comfortable with yourself. And to do that, you need to know who you are.

You start getting an image of who you are at a very early age. From the first time we are lying in a playpen, having a quiet suck on our big toe, and someone bends over us and says, "What a clever little boy!" we start filing away information about ourselves.

Since we haven't been in the world all that long, we assume that what we hear is The Truth. But we are not old enough to work out the things that we hear that really matter and the things that don't.

WHERE DOES YOUR SELF IMAGE COME FROM?

It comes from many different people and in all sorts of different ways.

1 It comes from your parents
When you are tiny, they tell you that you are, "Daddy's

little girl," or, "Mummy's big boy". As you grow up, you are likely to hear more *negative* comments than *positive* ones. This isn't because your family do not love you; it isn't because your teachers don't approve of you. It is because they are so busy trying to teach you to behave in the way they find acceptable that sometimes it all comes across as a lot of criticism.

There are times when you are painting a wonderful sunset with your finger-paints and your mother says, "You are so messy!" or you try to pour out your own Wheatybangs and spill the milk on your big sister's foot and she shrieks, "Why do you have to be so clumsy?" Someone gives you a beautiful new doll and you are speechless with delight. Then your mother says, "Say something – you are so rude!"

Pretty soon, you get the idea that you are messy, clumsy and rude. Of course, there have been plenty of times when you have been told that your painting is beautiful, that you are clever, funny and good. But most people remember negative comments and forget positive ones. Why? Because everyone, when they are young, wants to be loved and cherished and win approval from those near to them. When they are punished or deprived of things they want because they have done something that their parents see as being wrong, they think they may be deprived of the love and approval as well. Many people are punished for what they don't do, and not rewarded for what they do.

Sometimes even positive affirmations have a lasting effect on you. If you hear your mother repeatedly telling her friends, "Oh, Jenny is no trouble at all, bless her. Quiet as a mouse and so amenable!" you start thinking that being quiet and doing as you are told is A Very Good Thing. If you hear your father proudly telling his colleague, "It's wonderful – my son Mark is a chip off the old block; just like me – great kid!" you start thinking that doing what your father does and believing what he believes is the best way of being certain of his ongoing approval.

It can even happen with things we are good at: "Ian is the musical one", "Amanda is the academic one." Ian may long to be a world class footballer (and he may even be *better* at football than music) and Amanda may wish she could throw her history books away and do gymnastics all day, but because other people seem to see them in one way, they assume that is the only way they can be and that to change might be to risk losing the approval of those they want to impress. If your brother or sister is called "the musical one", you will automatically think that you are not musical and if they are constantly praised for being the life and soul of the party, you may think it is your role to remain on the sidelines.

2 It comes from big brothers and sisters

One day they are picking you up and telling you that you are cute and the next day they are laughing at you or calling you stupid because you can't do what they can do or you got a word wrong. When you are small, it is very easy to assume that everyone else has the world totally sussed and you are the one who can't get anything right.

Michelle is now 14 and when she was young, she and her big sister Nadine, who is two years older, would play Sailors together. *"We used to make boats out of cardboard boxes and I remember that after a while, Nadine would say that there was a storm at sea and I was drowning. She would push me out of my 'boat' and saying, 'You are almost dead.' A few minutes later, she would say, 'You are going to get eaten by a giant shark.' One day I said that it was her turn to die (because I was three, it really frightened me) and she said, 'No, people would miss me if I died.' I honestly thought for ages afterwards that no one would notice if I did."*

3 It comes from your teachers

Once you start school, a new factor contributes to the growth of your self image. Thomas, who is now 17, remembers constantly being compared to his brothers.

"I went to the same school as my three older brothers, who were all brilliant at sport and played in all the teams. I am totally uncoordinated and my games teacher used to say things like, 'You're not a patch on your brothers, are you?' and, 'Oh dear Thomas, the Browning talent certainly bypassed you!' I used to feel totally useless."

Melanie, now 18, had a similar problem. *"When I started secondary school, I was really miserable. My two best friends from primary school had left the area and I was lonely. I found the work difficult and because I was large for my age, I got teased. When I told my mum how awful it was, she said, 'It's a lovely school – your sisters adored it.' I wanted to scream and say, 'But I'm not them and I hate it.' "*

4 It comes from the media

It is very easy to be influenced by magazines and television. You pick up a magazine and there, on the cover, is drop dead gorgeous model, Dana, with huge blue eyes, perfect skin, bow shaped mouth and seductive gaze. And what do you think? "That's what I ought to look like. But I've got a turned up nose and crooked teeth – I look awful."

Or you see an advert for sun lotion. There is Lee, a guy with muscles to die for and a sun-tanned torso, cresting the waves on a surfboard while a clutch of admiring girls simper on the shoreline. And what do you think? "I haven't got a body like that and I'm useless at sport – I'll never get a girl!"

The problem is that what you are looking at doesn't exist. Magazine editors want perfection. Perfection does not exist. So they use a computer to create it. The computer wipes out Dana's bloodshot eyes, obliterates the pimple on her chin and adds a double dose of shine to her hair – and alters the colour slightly while it's at it.

The same computer makes Lee's muscles stand out rather more than they do, and because he is scared stiff of water it adds the surf and the sea afterwards. All he does is stand on a board in the studio.

These magazine images are not real. You are. What matters more than anything is that you start liking The Real You.

5 It comes from society

The culture within which you are brought up can affect your perception of yourself. Some Asian cultures expect women to be submissive to men; in Italian culture, children have far more freedom of speech and action than in the more reserved British culture.

6 It comes from your friends

As you grow up the greatest influence on the way you

see yourself comes from your friends. Few teenagers behave in the same way with their parents as they do with their friends. Even the words you use can be different when you are talking to your friends than they are when you are having a conversation with your parents. Quite often, you discover that the way your friends see you is totally different from the way your parents or teachers see you. And the way some of your friends see you will be different from how others do.

Fiona is Alice's best friend. *"Alice is really cool – she never gets fazed and is a brilliant listener. She comes up with great ideas and she's a real laugh."*

Penny is another of Alice's friends. *"Alice is really funny but she's so untidy! And of course, she'd forget her head if it wasn't screwed on!"*

Susan is in the same class as Alice. *"Alice is a bit of a swot – she's always worrying about her grades. She ought to lighten up a bit."*

They all see different sides to her, which are probably all correct. But whereas Susan sees Alice as being a bit too serious, her friends don't think that at all!

If Alice focuses on her untidiness and forgetfulness she will get one impression of herself and if she concentrates on her ability to make people laugh and work and play hard, she will get another. In the end, it is up to her.

7 It comes from your experiences
Sometimes things happen to us which affect the way we see ourselves.

Judi is now 15 and when she was very young, she suffered a lot of illness. Her family became very protective of her. *"I remember hearing them say that certain places were too crowded or too noisy or too dangerous for Judi,"* she recalls. *"For ages after I was better, I would think that anywhere with lots of people was somehow not safe for me. I believed I couldn't go out unless one of my family was with me and that if I mixed with lots of people something awful would happen to me."*

Liu is Chinese and has only lived in England for two years. *"When I came to live here, my English was not good and I made lots of mistakes. I found people laughed at what I said and so I tried to let others do all the talking. Now my English is much better but I still find it very hard to talk in a large group of people."*

So you can see how your self image will determine the way you behave, the type of friends you choose and the things you avoid.

YOU ARE NOT A TIN OF BAKED BEANS:
YOU DON'T NEED A LABEL!

When you shop in a supermarket, it is very convenient that all the goods have labels on. The label tells you what is in the tin or packet and how to deal with it when it's opened.

The problem with the labels that other people give us is that we believe them. We don't stop to think that inside Clumsy Clare lurks Clever, Caring and Compassionate Clare or that beneath Worried Wendy lurks Wendy the Wise and Witty.

It is worth remembering that labels can be peeled off and replaced. You are never stuck with what someone else has decided to call you.

Just as you may not realise until you take it out of the packet that the Giant Multi Topped Pizza you grabbed at in the supermarket had anchovies on top, so you may discover all sorts of surprising things hidden inside yourself.

Patrick had always been labelled "The timid one" in his family. His two brothers were really into watersports and rock climbing and Patrick preferred model-making and playing his saxophone. But when the family were out walking their dog, and a toddler slipped down a canal bank into the water, it was Patrick who jumped in after her.

"We never thought he had it in him," said his father. Patrick's courage was a "hidden ingredient" that everyone had omitted from his label.

Ghazala's family always spoke Urdu at home, and she was very shy of her halting English and native accent. All her friends thought of her as quiet and retiring and even a little bit dull and because of this she assumed she would never be included in any of the school plays. For two years, she helped backstage until one day, while rehearsals were going on, she began mimicking her teachers in mime. She was so brilliant at it that the following year, the head of English wrote a mime sketch into the production especially for her and Ghazala stole the show!

People often see only those parts of their friends or family that they are most interested in. Your mum, who wants you to become a Very Good Citizen, may notice your forgetfulness and untidiness. Your teacher, who is keen for you to be a Very Good Student, notices your flair for languages and your deftness with a hockey stick. Your best mate, who likes you as a Very Good

Friend, appreciates your sense of fun and the fact that you are willing to have a go at anything. They may all be right – but they are only seeing the bits of you that concern them the most.

By now, you are probably thinking that the way you see yourself today is not down to you at all. It is the fault of your parents and your relatives and your teachers and the media and the advertisers and... wrong! The only person who can decide how you see you is...YOU!

And sometimes it's not what other people say about you that affects the way you behave. It's what you say to yourself.

TALKING TO YOURSELF

You probably took one look at this section heading and thought, "Get real! I'm not crazy – I don't talk to myself." Oh yes you do. Everyone does.

There's the sort of furious under-the-breath muttering, "If my sister has taken my jeans again, I'll kill her."

There's the panic-stricken, "Oh no!" when you realise that you have left your biology project on the bus.

And there's the frantic chuntering behind the closed bedroom door, "It wasn't my fault, Dad, the football just took off through the window on its own," as you practise your best line in excuses.

But much more effective than all these chats with yourself are the messages you send to your sub-conscious without even thinking. Take a typical day.

You peer in the mirror in the morning.

"I look a mess," you tell yourself.

You give a wrong answer in class.

"I am so stupid," you say to yourself.

You miss a goal in basketball.

"I am totally useless," you think to yourself.

Your boyfriend dumps you.

"I am completely unlovable," you sob to yourself.

And your sub-conscious mind, which is very obedient and believes whatever it is asked to believe, takes all these messages on board and comes to the conclusion that you are messy, stupid, useless and unlovable. And since you believe this about yourself, you assume that everyone else will too.

It doesn't have to be like that. After all, you wouldn't be so hard on a friend, so why be thoroughly unfair to yourself?

Instead of looking for the flaws, why not look for the good things? Stand in front of the mirror and admire your beautiful grey eyes; remind yourself that last week it was you who scored the winning goal in the basketball match; and that while you are not too hot at history, you are a whiz at maths. As for the wandering boyfriend, tell yourself that now you are free to charm whoever takes your fancy.

And that same sub-conscious mind, still desperately keen to please, will come to the conclusion that you are attractive, sporty, clever and ready for romance, and set to work sending these messages out to the people you meet.

When you are faced with a new opportunity, the way you talk to yourself about it determines the way you will act. Without realising it, you say things like:

- I can't do that (because I might look silly).
- I can't risk attempting that (because I might fail).
- I won't try that (because I probably won't like it).
- I'd better pass on that (because I'll probably mess it up).
- I didn't succeed at that last time (so I won't try again).
- I'm useless at that (I made a mistake once).

Instead of berating yourself, try giving yourself some encouragement.

- I *can* do it!
- If I make a mistake, it won't be the end of the world.
- I'm getting better at that all the time.
- I'll do that – it looks like fun.

If you believe that people will be happy to meet you and pleased to become your friend, you are much more likely to draw them to you. If you go around thinking you are rubbish, and that no one in their right mind would want to have anything to do with you, they will pick up those vibes and start acting that way.

That's easy to say – but not so easy to put into practice! So just how do you give yourself a Good Talking To instead of a Bad Mouth Session?

You wake up to find a large zit on your chin.
Don't tell yourself: This zit is the pits; I look a complete nerd; everyone will notice – I am hideous.
Do say: At least it's not on my nose, and with green concealer it's practically invisible.

You go into a maths exam with a large number of overactive butterflies in your stomach.

Don't tell yourself: I am useless at maths; I am bound to fail; oh, no, number 3 is impossible – I might as well give up now.

Do tell yourself: I've done heaps of revision and I might as well give it my best shot. There must be some bits I can do.

You are taking part in a class discussion about vivisection. You know that your best friend is against it but you think it is an essential part of medical research.

Don't tell yourself: I'm usually wrong anyway and besides, he'll hate me if I argue so I'll just shut up.

Do tell yourself: I have a right to my own opinions and as long as I accept his, I have the right to express them too.

Expressing your opinion is the first big step to total confidence.

So just what does being confident really mean?

What it means	*What it doesn't mean*
Liking yourself for who you are.	Assuming you are more important than anyone else.
Acknowledging your feelings.	Pretending to be something you are not.
Knowing what you want and working to achieve it.	Riding roughshod over other people.
Thinking positively.	Putting other people down.

Behaving skilfully.	Expecting other people to sort out your problems for you.
Stating your opinions clearly.	Refusing to admit when you are wrong.

You don't learn confidence overnight. Most people get a little more confident with each year that goes by and with every challenge they manage to meet and overcome. There may be no shortcuts to *being* totally confident, but there are clever ways in which you can make others *believe* you are confident.

It's all down to body language.

TAKE YOUR FINGER OUT OF YOUR EAR WHEN YOU ARE TALKING TO ME! – body language

Your body can be your best friend or your worst enemy when it comes to sending out messages to people you meet. The way you stand, the expression on your face and the gestures you make all give people ideas about who you are and what you are like. And the great news is that you are in charge of the picture they get!

Body language, or non-verbal communication, is going on all the time, even when you are not aware of it. You can get an immediate feeling about a person you have never spoken to. You may see someone and instantly think, "That's an unhappy kid," or, "I bet she has a wicked temper." What you are doing is picking up the unspoken clues given out by their facial expression, the way they stand orthe way they move.

Every part of the body is important and you can use it to help you seem calmly in control even when your knees are knocking and your heart is thumping!

1 The eyes have it!

• *Make eye contact* with someone else in the room. If you stand with your head down, or gaze out of the window, you look disinterested and unfriendly and people will be more inclined to ignore you.

• *Keep eye contact* during a conversation. This makes you appear sincere, while if you keep looking away you can look shifty or bored. Eye contact encourages the other person to talk to you – and the more they say, the less you have to!

2 Face facts!

• *Smile!* Not only does a grin make you feel more relaxed but it sends out messages that here is someone who is easy to get on with.

• *Keep smiling!* During conversations, smiles and nods give the speaker the impression that you find them interesting and amusing. Smiles are positive: frowns, sighs and staring at the floor are all negative. But this doesn't mean you have to fix an inane grin on your face!

3 Limber up!

• When you are nervous or shy, it is sometimes difficult to stand still. You shift your weight from one foot to another, nibble a fingernail and twiddle with a strand of hair. Not only does this send out non-confident messages to others, it makes you feel worse by the minute. Instead, let your arms hang loosely at your side or hold them loosely in front of you – arms folded across can make you look stand-offish; use hand gestures (movement is relaxing and expressive) or hold a glass to stop yourself fiddling; and always look interested (which is very flattering for your companion).

• To help yourself feel confident, keep your back straight, your head up and put a bounce in your step!

• Stand with you legs straight rather than crossed. If you're sitting down, don't lean right back in your chair, it's better to sit forward with your legs uncrossed – that way you look more open and interested.

4 Spaced out!

• Everyone needs their personal space. If you know someone really well and like them a lot, you will feel quite comfortable being as close as 18 inches to them. But if you have only just met them, and are still forming an opinion, you are much more likely to stand a metre away from them. If someone invades that personal space, you feel threatened. So remember not to crowd anyone you have just met – you will only come across as pushy. But don't retreat too far or they will assume you are cold and disinterested.

Many famous actors, as well as students at RADA and other stage schools, have discovered the benefits of the Alexander Technique, which not only promotes good posture, but helps you to use your body to exude confidence. Like all therapies you need to be taught by a qualified practitioner, but learning how to release tension from your body can make you feel as well as look a whole heap more in control.

Chapter 3
• •

LOOK WHO'S TALKING!:
making conversation

"No man would listen to you talk if he didn't know it was his turn next."
Ed Howe, American journalist (1853-1937)

FIRST WORDS

When you were a baby and wanted something really badly, you had a problem. You couldn't say, "Excuse me, but I quite fancy a mashed banana with double toffee ice cream and sprinkles to go." All you could do was take a deep breath and yell as loudly as possible. This made people stop what they were doing and hover over you with anxious expressions, but they still hadn't a clue whether you were after the mashed banana, a dry nappy, a quick burst of Hickory Dickory Dock or a big hug.

Sometimes they thought it was wind and other times they tried putting you to bed because they were tired. And the ice cream stayed in the fridge and you had no way of telling them.

But then you learned a few words. Now you could say, "Drink" when you were thirsty. OK, it was a bit of a lottery as to whether you got milk or juice or just plain boring water, but it was progress. The more words you learned, the greater your chances of having your needs met. Words, you discovered, had power.

As you got older, there were times when you were scared, or worried, or just plain uncomfortable and you tried to tell them about it.

"There's a monster in my wardrobe," you sobbed when you were three.

"Everybody at school is horrid to me," you whispered when you were seven.

"I'm worried that no one will ever fancy me," you confessed when you were twelve.

What happened?

"Don't be such a silly boy!" your big brother said, opening the wardrobe and proving you wrong.

"Of course they're not!" your father insisted, even though he wasn't in the playground when the gang took your Smarties.

"You should have more important things to worry about!" your mother insisted, as if what was important to her had to matter most to you too.

So you began to think that your views and feelings were somehow not quite up to scratch and it might, after all, be best not to say too much about them. And that's when those first seeds of shyness were sown; when you began to feel shy of admitting how you felt or what you thought.

And because you haven't had much practice at conversation skills, those seeds of doubt start growing. When you find yourself facing the first day at a new school, or joining a club or being introduced to someone new at a party, they sprout into very big and very real fears. You start thinking, "What if?"

- What if everyone thinks I'm stupid?
- What if that drop dead gorgeous guy I've been fancying for weeks ignores me totally?
- What if no one takes any notice of me?
- What if I say the wrong thing?
- What if they laugh at me?
- What if no one even bothers to listen?

By the time you have considered all the things that could go wrong if you opened your mouth, saying nothing seems a very attractive option!

But it would be very lonely to stay silent for ever. What you need is A Strategy!

SHY-BUSTING STRATEGIES FOR THE FIRST SIXTY SECONDS

The first sixty seconds after meeting someone new can be awful. But there are things you can do to help.

1 Forget about yourself

This is the most difficult, which is why it comes first. Once you've done this, the rest is a doddle! Try to ignore the way you feel, how you think you look or the impression you want to make. Concentrate on what is going on around you. You remember how when you feel ill and curl up in front of a good movie on television, the pain gets less during the exciting bits? It doesn't really. You just forget about it because something more interesting has taken over. Think about how shy you are and you will feel awful. Think of something else – how good the band is, or whether

Dave really fancies Melissa or is secretly yearning after Chloe – and you will cope much better.

2 Banish fear with focus

When those feelings of fear start to take over, focus all your attention on the person you have just met. If they are talking, listen intently to what they are saying; say things like, "That's really interesting – what happened next?" which makes you sound interested and the other person feel accepted. If they are as tongue-tied as you, try saying, "I never know what to say when I meet someone new". They will be relieved and might even admit to feeling the same, and you will both relax.

3 Look friendly

The easiest way to do this is to look at other people when you talk to them (this doesn't mean staring, of course). It is very tempting for someone who is shy to examine the floor in great detail, or scrutinise their thumbnail, or look at the far wall – anything rather than risk eye contact. To the other person, this looks as if you are being unfriendly and have no real interest in them. They feel rejected and begin to back off and you end up telling yourself that it is because you are so boring.

4 Pretend it's not you who is shy

This is a clever way of deceiving your sub-conscious mind. Tell yourself that it is the other guy who is the shy one. Then imagine how they feel – which won't be difficult because you've felt it yourself. Try as hard as you can to put them at their ease in just the same way as you would like people to behave with you. It really

works; you find you forget your own self-conscious-
ness because you have set yourself a challenge.

5 Take some breathing space

How often have you been told to, "Take a deep breath
and start again"? This is not accident. In the time it
takes to inhale, hold your breath and gently exhale,
you can collect your thoughts, relax your jaw and
think one beautiful thought! One 13-year-old I know
thinks of his red setter, another of the day she scored
four goals for the county junior hockey squad. I
pretend my best friend is lurking behind the door,
giving me one of her wicked grins and the thumbs-up
sign! It works wonders – especially on those days
when you think that everyone else in the room is better
than you are.

6 Talk in sentences

It is so easy when you feel shy to say "Yes" and "No"
in response to questions. But it doesn't get you very far.
Look at this example:

Kate: Hi! You're Louise, aren't you?
You: Yes.
Kate: You must be a friend of Annabel's?
You: Yes.
Kate: Do you go to Middlehampton High?
You: Yes.
Kate: My brother goes there – Tim Poole. Do you
know him?
You: No.

Doesn't get you very far, does it?

Now try it this way.

Kate: Hi, I'm Kate – you're Louise, aren't you?
You: Yes – are you a friend of Annabel's?
Kate: Yes, we both belong to the same drama club.
You: Really? Have you been in plays together?
Kate: Last year I was Bottom and she was Titania in *A Midsummer Night's Dream*, and it was so funny because at the dress rehearsal, this guy who was playing Oberon...

And suddenly you have a conversation. Kate thinks you are great because you are interested in what she does, and all you have to do is look suitably impressed and amused at intervals. Which leads us on to the next strategy.

7 Don't panic if you blush

Of all the outward signs of shyness, the one people worry about most is blushing. Everyone does it at some time or another, but the more self-conscious you are, the more readily you will blush. "I blush because I am embarrassed," you tell yourself. But in fact, it is often the reverse – you are embarrassed because you are blushing – and worrying about it makes you blush more.

Lorna is 14 and went through a stage when she blushed very easily. *"Then one day I decided to say to myself that even if I felt my face getting hot, I would carry on as if nothing had happened. The first time I tried it, I asked this girl I was with to tell me about her new Labrador puppy – and by the time I had finished laughing at his antics, the blush had faded. I'm not saying I never blush these days – but at least by using this trick, I don't worry about it any more."*

8 Take an interest

People love talking about the things that give them a buzz. If you know the guy you have just met plays ice hockey, get him talking on the subject. That does not mean you have to know anything about the sport; a simple question like, "Do you train a great deal?" will set him going and immediately he will think you are a cool person. If you haven't a clue what someone enjoys, try saying, "Have you seen the new Sean Bean movie yet?" or even, "Do you live round here?"

9 Know your subject

Do you and your best friend talk non-stop? Does your family ever tell you to shut up? You are not shy then, so when you are stuck for something to say, think about how you feel at home. What is it you chat on about to your brothers and sisters and to your friends? Find the thing that fires you with enthusiasm and you have a topic with which to start the conversational ball rolling.

10 End on a positive note

Sometimes you manage to get into a conversation with someone new and are just beginning to relax and unwind, when her best friend bowls up and starts talking nineteen to the dozen. If your new friend doesn't introduce you say something like, "Hi, I'm Sally – I've just met Eleanor – and you are...?"

If, as sometimes happens, they go off together, say, "It was great talking to you," – that leaves them with a positive image and makes you less likely to feel dumped.

11 Make an effort

If you are at that awful stage when you are stuck in the corner of the room, clutching a wedge of pepperoni pizza and a glass of Lilt and feeling like a spare part, focus on the friendliest looking person in the room. Or find someone who is also on their own. When you make eye contact, smile. Even if nothing happens, the smile will make you look approachable and you'll feel more cheerful. And if *everyone* is talking in groups, go up to the least scary looking group. If they're friendly, they'll probably start chatting to you anyway, but if they're absorbed in conversation, listen and look interested – you'll probably be able to ask a question or contribute at some point.

So far so good. Now just imagine this. You are at a party, quite happy with your own group of friends, when across the room you see this drop dead gorgeous guy and he is looking at you. With interest. He starts to move towards you.

And you grab your bag and flee to the loo. And spend the rest of the evening wishing you had known how to handle it. You might be surprised to discover that he was just the tiniest bit relieved to see you disappear. Both of you are afraid of the same thing: rejection. But it doesn't have to be like that.

TALKING TO MEMBERS OF THE OPPOSITE SEX

Talking to members of the opposite sex should not, in theory, be any more difficult than talking to people of your own sex. In practice, it is often much harder, especially if you fancy them. Why?

• Because you think of them as a different species.
• Because you are convinced that your success or failure with the opposite sex is a sign of your own worth or lack of it.
• Because you don't know what sort of things interest them.
• Because you think of them as *boy* friends or *girl* friends, instead of simply friends.
• Because you think your own friends might make fun of you.
• Because you are scared of being rejected.

Before you exchange one word with each other, all sorts of anxieties hurtle through your mind.

What goes through Jake's mind:	*What goes through Tina's mind:*
That girl looks friendly – maybe I'll go over.	Oh my God! He's looking at me!
Oh, she's looked away – she probably thinks I'm a nerd.	My hair's a mess – does my breath smell? Why isn't he moving?
She looked at me! I think I'll give it a go.	He's coming! Keep calm.
What shall I say?	What shall I say?

I could say, "Hi, want some action?" No, that's naff.

I could say...oh no, what shall I say?

Perhaps she's already got a guy.

He's probably been with loads of girls.

Someone like her won't be interested in me.

Someone like him won't want me.

I'll just get a drink.

I'll just dash to the loo.

Both Jake and Tina were so worried about the impression they might make that in the end they passed up on the chance to get to know one another.

Tips for talking to boys

There are an awful lot of myths flying around – boys only want to go out with pretty girls, boys avoid girls with brains, boys are only after one thing. All of which are nonsense – that's like saying all cats are black or every car is a Porsche. When you meet a guy you want to know better, forget about him being male and just see him as another person.

1 Don't worry too much about making a super stunning impact. It's natural that you want him to think you are utterly captivating, but if you think so much about the impression you are making, chances are you will make the wrong one! You can act coy – and end up looking silly; talk non-stop and bore the poor guy rigid; or come on too strong and frighten him to death. If you apply the usual rules of smile, question and listen, you will give him the one thing guys cannot exist without – flattery!

2 Try to find out what turns him on (apart from you!) and then ask his opinion. If he is soccer mad, ask what he thinks Little Trottington's chances are in the Middleshire league; if he is the leading light of the school drama club, ask him what his dream role would be. When people talk about the things closest to their heart, they become enthusiastic and relaxed and afterwards, they think of you as being someone easy to talk to.

3 Forget all that talk about boys being really sure of themselves. Sure, there are some guys who drip self-confidence from every pore – but then, there are girls like that too. Boys like you to think they are super-cool dudes, and they work hard at preserving that image, even with their own mates – but underneath most of them are just as unsure of themselves as girls.

4 If he asks you out, don't say, "Great! When? Where? What time?" He probably hasn't thought that far ahead! Much better to say, "I would really enjoy that – it's been great talking to you." And if you decide that you don't want to see him again, don't just say, "No thanks". He will feel that you have rejected his invitation because of some fault of his own. Instead, say something like, "Thank you for asking but the next few weeks are hectic for me – maybe later in the term?"

By then, he will have found someone else!

5 Don't imagine that just because you don't rate yourself as particularly pretty, guys won't fancy you. A pretty face may be an initial attraction, but no matter how beautiful a girl may be, if she isn't fun to be with, caring and friendly, there's no mileage in the relationship. Do you only go for guys with film star looks? Or do you want them to have a wicked sense of humour and an interest in something other than themselves? It's the same for boys!

They find it just as hard to know what to say to you as you do thinking up chat up lines for them. It isn't a contest; you don't get extra marks for clever comebacks.

Sometimes, trying to be clever can make the other person feel inferior – and that's inexcusable.

What he says: Fancy a dance?
What he may be thinking: Please God, don't let her say no.
Don't say: I might – if you try to ask nicely.
Do say: Thank you – I'd like that.

What he says: You're really pretty!
What he may be thinking: And I bet you won't give me a second glance.
Don't say: No I'm not.
Do say: Thank you – what a nice thing to say.

What he says: I suppose you've had loads of boyfriends.
What he may be thinking: You'll be much more experienced than me.

Don't say: Too many to count!
Do say: One or two – but no one special.

What he says: I'm going stock car racing on Saturday.
What he may be thinking: Dare I ask you to come along too?
Don't say: Booooring!
Do say: That's something I've never done – what happens?

What he says: We could go out somewhere tonight.
What he may be thinking: As long as it's cheap.
Don't say: Mega! How about the Chinese followed by a film and a night club?
Do say: I'd love that; why don't we go halves on seeing that new Keanu Reeves film?

What he says: You're OK, you know that?
What he may be thinking: I'm totally completely head over in heels in love.
Don't say: Only OK?
Do say: I think you're pretty all right too!

Boys have just as many hang-ups as girls; they feel quite safe standing in a huddle at a party, ogling girls across the room. But single one out and try to strike up a conversation and you will probably get a quick mumble before they sidle back to the safety of the group. This is because their fears are not so very different from your own.

• They think you look gorgeous – and assume you will reject them! Many boys are so frightened of looking like the biggest loser if they ask you for a date and you refuse – that they don't bother asking in the first place. Just as you think, "He'd never be interested in someone like me," he thinks, "Who'd want to go out with a guy like me?"

• They are scared! Girls do mature before boys and if you are attractive with a great figure, loads of designer gear and oodles of confidence, they may feel you are out of their league. That doesn't mean you have to go around looking like a slob, but you might find that when you are in your school uniform and following the "No make-up, no jewellery" rule, you get more invitations out than when you have spent three hours in front of the mirror. Life just isn't fair!

• They worry that they don't know good chat up lines/how to kiss super-sexily/how to make you fancy them. Boys may brag about their prowess with girls but that's usually because they don't want their mates to make fun of them. They think that fantasising is a lot safer than the risk of trying the real thing!

Boys bitch too!
They say that girls can be bitchy – but boys do their fair share of slagging too. And it doesn't always mean they detest the sight of you!

There can be all sorts of reasons:

• You've just turned him down – and he can't take the rejection.
• He feels insecure and assumes that putting you down will make him look macho.
• He likes the feeling of power it gives him to make you upset.

• He feels guilty about having dumped you and wants to make it sound as if it was all your fault.
• He's scared of your cool sophistication!
• He's jealous because you fancy his best mate – and not him.

It can be pretty hurtful to hear unkind things being said about you by the guy you thought, just probably, cared. But there are ways of handling it and coming out looking cool.

• Ignore his taunts. If he persists, ask him why he is doing it. He will be so stunned to find you are challenging him rather than dissolving in a heap, that he will probably stop in mid-slag!
• Don't let him see you are upset because then he will think he has won. And don't take it too personally – it will be someone else's turn next week!
• Get your friends to stand up for you. No boy wants to find himself loathed by every available girl in town!
• Don't slag back. It's fine to say, "Get lost!" but don't start a major character assassination in front of the entire class.
• Say, "It's a shame a great guy like you can't think of anything more memorable to say."
• Remember that any boy who spends their time slating girls is mega-sad and find yourself a guy who has too much savvy to slag!

Tips for talking to girls

1   Girls in groups can be pretty scary – they giggle and gossip a lot. If you want to talk to a girl, it's a very good idea to get her on her own.

2   Because first words are so hard, a clever ploy is to come in with an offer of help. "I see your glass is empty – can I get you a drink?" "Can I put your violin up on the rack for you?" or, "I've got a book that might be really useful for your history assignment – may I lend it to you?"

3   Girls worry just as much as boys about the way they look, so early on it is a good idea to pay her a compliment. It can be as general as, "You look terrific"; you don't have to embark on a paean in praise of her green eyes, auburn locks and pearly white teeth!

4   One of the difficulties for both of you is handling the embarrassment of wondering what to say next. To deflect attention away from each other, start talking about something else. If you are at a party, make a comment about the music or other people who are there; if you are at school, ask whether the other person is involved in a particular sports event or play.

5   Don't try to be clever. It's easy to want to copy the cool chat up lines you hear in the TV soaps – but very often they come across as just that; copies of someone else's script! A girl is not interested in how good your memory is – merely in how sincere you are.

6 Don't fall into the trap of thinking that you have to be macho or laddish. Most girls are turned off by coarse or suggestive language and noisy "look at me" behaviour.

7 Believe her when she says no. You don't have to kiss on a first date; if she feels uncomfortable with any part of your behaviour, respect her wishes and back off. You'll be the winner in the long run because most girls appreciate a guy who recognises their right to set their own pace.

8 Never, ever talk about your past relationships with a girl you are trying to chat up! She is not interested in how Miranda Appleby fell at your feet, or whether the whole of Year Ten was pining for you when you were off with a rugby injury. What she needs to know is that you are interested in her – not merely adding to your list of romantic conquests!

In the end, the same rule applies: be yourself!

TALKING TO ADULTS

Other people's parents can be pretty intimidating at times, especially if you have never met them before. It can be tempting just to grunt a quick, "Hi!" and dash up the stairs two at a time to your mate's room or to mumble an answer to their question while gazing steadfastly at your feet. The funny thing is that most adults really want to make a good impression on their children's friends – some so much that they try to be terribly hip and ask you what you think of the latest recording by a band whose name they have just memorised from the chart lists at the back of their daily newspaper! They think that by chatting to you they will make you feel at ease – and if you try to chat back, you will find it works!

1 Don't just say, "Yes" or, "No" when they ask you a question. If they ask if you had a good holiday, say something like, "We had a great time in Cornwall – have you been there?" or, "It was brilliant – how was your trip to Venice?"

2 If there is an awkward silence, make a friendly comment. "It's really kind of you to invite me to supper," or, "Jake tells me you are house-hunting – how is it going?" It usually only takes one sentence to unleash a conversation and your friend's parents are left thinking what a great guy you are!

3 Don't be put off when they quiz you. If they don't know you too well, and you are about to take their daughter out on a date, they may well want details. It may sound like the Spanish Inquisition, but rather than being curt and offhand, give them honest answers. If they ask your plans for the evening, tell them. "We're going to see a film and have a pizza, and we should be back by 11pm," will go down much better than a shrug of the shoulders and a muttered, "Dunno".

4 Remember that a smile is a great ice-breaker. However shy you are, you can muster a broad grin! When meeting someone for the first time, or talking to people older than you, always remember that the first thing they look at is your face. If they are greeted with a friendly smile, they immediately warm to the wearer and are likely to start a conversation themselves.

5 Leave a good impression. If you are going out, turn and say goodbye to your friend's parents. If they have plied you with coke and crisps, thank them for the snack. And ending on a friendly note – "See you again soon, I hope," or, "Good luck with the golf," means that you will be flavour of the month in that household for some time to come!

Chapter 4

. . . .

FIGHTING TALK

"No man can think clearly when his fists are clenched."
George Jean Nathan, American critic (1882-1958)

Anger is a very powerful emotion and one that scares most people. It isn't just shy people who have problems expressing anger; it applies to almost everyone at some time. Some people do it *too* easily and others not at all and both these extremes can be harmful.

HOW DOES ANGER BUILD UP?

1 The first flush

You discover that your best friend has told your deepest secret to half of Year Nine; you get blamed by your teacher for something you didn't do; your dad says you can't go to the disco of the year and when you ask why, he says, "Because I say so!"; your parents keep rowing and when you ask what's up, they tell you to mind your own business.

All these things can make you very, very angry or upset – and that anger and unhappiness is justified:

Your friend told a secret – and that broke your trust.
You got blamed wrongly – and that was unjust.

Your dad said no – and you deserve an explanation.

You were worried by your parents' fighting – and couldn't get an explanation.

Your feelings of anger can make you clench your fists, turn your legs to jelly and make your stomach lurch. You may want to burst into tears, or scream or throw something across the room. And after this First Flush, you might begin to feel rather guilty for your reactions.

You don't need to feel guilty. It is OK to feel cross and cheated and let down as long as you do something about it. What you want to avoid if you possibly can is:

2 The silent simmer

This is the period of time when you brood on your anger. Sometimes you have no choice: it simply isn't convenient to say anything. If you stood up in the middle of biology and shouted, "I'll get you for this, Kirsty Hopkins!" you would only make a fool of yourself and get detention for Behaviour Unbecoming. If your mother is entertaining the vicar, you can hardly hurtle into the sitting room and shriek, "How *could* you tell Mandy's mother that I suck my thumb in bed?"

Sometimes you turn your fury over and over in your mind because you don't know what to do about it. You may decide to suppress it – or you may choose to express it. The way you act is likely to be influenced by the way you have been brought up.

DEALING WITH ANGER

1 Do your bury your anger and hope it will go away?

If you were encouraged to bottle up your feelings and never let your fury show, you may find it difficult to tell anyone that you are even slightly miffed, never mind so angry you could spit bullets. Or maybe you remember that when you did make your feelings known, it landed you in trouble. After all, most people recall being punished for saying, "Granny, you smell horrible," – even if she *was* reeking of garlic and mothballs at the time, or being told, "Nice little girls don't argue". If you feel like this, you may choose the Buttoned Lip Approach, biting your tongue, counting to ten and then going upstairs and punching the wall.

Suppressing your feelings makes for a quiet life at the time, and on occasions it is the politest thing to do. But do it all the time and you lay up a whole bundle of trouble in the future. All that happens is that the resentment builds up inside you and the real problem, which might have been quite small to begin with, grows and grows until it threatens to take over.

Remember:

• If you choose to let people walk all over you, you mustn't complain when you turn into a doormat.
• If you really believe that what you feel doesn't matter, you mustn't be surprised when everyone else takes that view too.
• If you think that everyone takes notice of the other guys and no one is ever going to want to listen to you, then sure as anything that is what will happen.

2 Do you fly off the handle and expect everyone to take notice?

If you grew up in a family where expressing anger was an everyday occurrence and where people thought nothing of shouting about their feelings, it may mean that even if you are just the tiniest bit niggled, you blow your top and launch into a mega slanging match. Maybe you discovered that the only way to be heard was to shout louder and longer than everyone else. In the end, you expended just as much energy demanding a custard cream instead of a chocolate digestive as you would in expressing fury at your younger brother who had just ridden your new mountain bike into a brick wall. In which case you might go for Verbal Volcanics.

This is when all the anger and frustration erupts without any sort of form or shape or thought and like natural volcanoes, it can be pretty destructive.

You find yourself saying things like:

"I hate you!"

"You've ruined everything."

"How could you be such a jerk?"

"I wish I'd never met you!"

"Get out of my life!"

These sort of responses are usually spat out, or shouted, or snarled through curling lips. You might feel better for about ten seconds but you won't achieve anything, and the object of your anger will simply shout back or turn tail and disappear. All very counter productive.

You may attract more short-term attention by being aggressive. But it won't be the sort of attention that brings results – not for long anyway. If you choose to be aggressive, remember:

• If you shout long and loud, people get bored. They become immune to your anger – and when you do want to say how you feel about something seriously important, no one takes any notice.

• If you become aggressive, you often lose control of your emotions and get irrational. Then people lose respect for you and stop listening even to the loudest of yells.

• If you jump off the handle immediately, you're not giving the person who made you angry a chance to explain.

3 The right way to deal with anger

You may think that it is easier to say nothing and just let other people do what they want. You may think forcing your opinions and emotions on others works fine. But it is more likely that you would prefer people to listen to the way you feel, and then respect your needs.

There is no harm in admitting that you feel angry as long as you tell the other person why in a way that encourages him or her to listen, understand and hopefully choose to do something about it.

• Admit responsibility for your anger – say, "*I* am angry because you broke my new wraparound sunspecs," rather than, "*You* are the clumsiest clod in Year Ten."

• Acknowledge the problem, but don't reject the person who caused it. Say to your parents, "I feel really annoyed that you won't let me go to the Manic Mayhem concert," not, "You two are the most rotten parents on the face of this earth."

• Listen to the other person's response and acknowledge what they say. That doesn't mean you have to agree. You can say, "I hear what you are saying but I still feel very upset by your attitude."

By talking about the *problem* and not the *person*, you are less likely to keep an argument going.

The way you feel	*Constructive anger*	*Destructive anger*
Angry and let down by your friend.	I feel hurt that you betrayed my trust like that.	You're a cow and I never want to speak to you again.
Misjudged and unfairly blamed.	I didn't do that, and I would like the chance to prove it.	You're always picking on me.
Fobbed off with no explanation.	I'm angry that you won't tell me why. I need to know.	You just hate to see me having fun.
Scared and angry at being excluded.	I am worried by your arguments and need to know what is going on.	You two are pathetic.

See the difference? When you express your anger constructively, you take responsibility for the way you feel. When you use it destructively, you merely hurl accusations at the other person, which puts their back up and makes them even less responsive to your needs. People who learn to handle anger constructively are more likely to get at least some of what they want and much more likely to feel good about themselves and their behaviour.

4 When you are so angry you can't speak

There are times when you are so mad that you cannot trust yourself to say a word. You know you have to get things sorted but you also know you need to calm down before you do. Try the following:

• Count to ten – in French or backwards if necessary!
• Write it all down in a letter. This clarifies your thoughts and if you read it back to yourself – out loud – you will find the bits that really are too over the top!
• Take some slow, deep breaths and concentrate on relaxing those clenched fists and puckered lips.
• Take some immediate and energetic exercise – punch a cushion, run as fast as you can round the block, do twenty press-ups or shadow box.
• Make yourself think of three nice things about the person you are angry with. This is a neat way of dissipating the sort of rage that flares up because of one thing they have done because it reminds you of all the things about them you still love.

SO JUST HOW GOOD ARE YOU AT HARNESSING HOSTILITY?

1 Whenever you go out with Trudi, she is always late.

This time you have been waiting outside the cinema for half an hour in the rain. When she does turn up, and you ask her what happened, she just says, "It's no big deal". You feel furious. Do you say:
a) "I feel it is – I am freezing. Next time, I'll go in and you can join me later"?
b) "That's the last time I ever go out with you and that's final"?
c) "That's fine – I must have made a mistake over the time"?

2 Ravinder keeps borrowing things from you and forgetting to give them back. Right now he has two books, your video of *Waterworld* and your cycle helmet. Now he wants to borrow your rollerblades. You really want to use them yourself this weekend. Do you say:
a) "Not likely, you thief!"?
b) "All right," and cancel your rollerblading session?
c) "I need them right now, but if you give me back the rest of my stuff, you could borrow them next Friday"?

3 A group of you are having a debate about blood sports. Craig says that you are a softie because you think fox hunting is cruel. Do you say:
a) "I respect your viewpoint, but I truly believe the sport should be banned"?
b) "Well, I suppose you could be right"?
c) "If that's what you think, you are a cruel sadist and I don't want anything more to do with you"?

4 You are feeling really miserable about something and a friend asks what is wrong. You are simply not ready to tell anyone. Do you say:

a) "Stop interfering and leave me alone!"?
b) "It's really kind of you to ask but I would rather not talk about it right now"?
c) "Nothing"?

5 Your father is in a bad mood about your school grades. He says you should be doing better, but you know that you are trying your hardest. Do you say:
a) "Sorry," and go upstairs to have a little worry?
b) "I find maths and science really hard, but I am doing my best – and my French and geography is much better this term"?
c) "Well, you're a fine one to talk; you left school without any qualifications, didn't you?" and storm out of the room?

Answers:

1 a) 3. You have given Trudi a reason for your anger and a positive course of action for the next time.

b) 1. You are risking the loss of a friendship because you object to one facet of her behaviour.

c) 0. By taking responsibility for something that was not your fault, you pave the way for your friend to continue to disregard your feelings.

2 a) 1. He is not a thief, merely forgetful.

b) 0. Giving in is no way to prevent the same problem arising again.

c) 3. You have given a valid reason for your refusal, and conditions on which you will reconsider.

3 a) 3. You have not slated their opinion, merely re-stated your own.

b) 0. You do not believe they are right so don't compromise yourself by pretending that you do.

c) 1. This is aggressive, unpleasant and completely unnecessary.

4 a) 1. You have rebuffed a perfectly friendly approach without giving any reason.

b) 3. You acknowledge your friend's concern and state your own need for privacy.

c) 0. Since your friend has eyes and can see that something is wrong, your denial only makes her feel rejected.

5 a) 0. You have a view and a right to state it.

b) 3. By acknowledging your weakness and drawing attention to your strengths, you will gain respect and help.

c) 1. Drawing attention to your father's academic failings when your own performance is under discussion is likely to make him more entrenched in his attitude.

Scoring

10-15   You have the confidence to express your feelings when angry or upset and people are likely to listen to what you have to say.

6-9   Blaming other people for things that are wrong in your life may seem an easy way out but it won't earn you any Brownie points.

0-5   You run the risk of becoming a doormat. You have as much right to express your feelings as anyone else so take a deep breath and fight your corner!

COOL IT! – seven sure-fire ways of reining in your wrath

Before you launch into a diatribe of how badly you feel, remember that there are no winners and losers when it comes to giving criticism or expressing hurt. The aim is for *both* of you to feel better at the end of the conversation than you did at the start.

1 Explain what you are angry about

Stomping round the room with a purple face and clenched fists lets everyone know that you are cross – but there isn't much they can do about it because they don't know why. If they ask what is wrong, avoid saying things like:

• "Well, if you don't know why I feel like this, there's no point discussing it." (If you won't discuss it, they can't help.)
• "It's just – oh, everything. OK?" (Like global warming? The price of leggings? The plight of the lesser spotted newt in inland waterways?)
• "What do you care!" (Enough to ask in the first place.)
• "You know perfectly well what's wrong so don't pretend you don't!" (If they knew, they wouldn't have asked.)

If they don't ask what is wrong, say that you feel really upset and would like to talk it through. Then state quite calmly what has annoyed you. Don't accuse them of being responsible for your anger (even if something they have said or done has upset you).

Don't say	*Do say*
You make me mad the way you are always late.	I was really pleased when you suggested coming bowling, but I feel angry because I have been waiting in the cold for half an hour.
You never have time for me.	I'd really like to see more of you but you always seem to have so many things to do.
You went off with Megan and left me out.	I feel upset because I thought we were going to go shopping together.
You are always so horrid to me.	I couldn't believe that you really meant those things you said, and that is why I am upset.

2 Don't get dramatic

You may feel genuinely upset or hurt by someone's actions but it doesn't help to say, "You have ruined my entire life!" or, "Now you've said I'm fat, I shall never eat again." If you get into the habit of saying things that are over-dramatic or patently untrue, you lose credibility with your friends and they start automatically switching off – so when you say something that really does have importance, they have developed the habit of not listening.

3 Don't drag up old issues

If you are angry with your friend for borrowing your bike without asking, say so. Don't add, "And last week you took my atlas and the week before you spilt cola all over my history folder." Remember that your friend is human; he won't thank you for raking over all his faults and failings and he is far less likely to take on board what you say about the bicycle if he feels that all you are doing is reeling off a catalogue of grievances.

4 Don't resort to sarcasm

When you feel hurt and cross, it is very easy to lash out and say things you don't really mean but which will be remembered by the other person long after you have forgotten them. Remarks such as, "Sorry? Is that all you can say – sorry?" or, "I should have known better than to lend my suede slingbacks to a dork with two left feet," only serve to make things worse.

5 Criticise the behaviour, not the person

Name-calling is childish and achieves nothing. Say, "I am annoyed that you ate all my chocolates," rather than, "You greedy fat pig!"

6 Don't screech, and listen to the other person

Consciously lower your voice. Screaming and shouting has far less effect than speaking quietly. If you drop your voice, the other person has to listen harder and automatically pays greater attention. When you have made your case, listen. If you feel that you are the injured party it is all too easy to rant and rave and not let the other person have their say. Give them the chance to offer an explanation or to apologise. By affording them the right of reply, you maintain your dignity. If you don't, this can happen:

You: I feel so angry – you didn't turn up for the tennis match and I had to pull out.
Paul: I know, you see...
You: Oh, that's right, wriggle out of it. You just can't be relied on, you...
Paul: What happened was...
You: What happened was that you, as usual, couldn't be bothered.
Paul: Actually, we got a phone call to say my gran had died.
You: Oh – sorry.

6 Don't give up
If the other person tries to change the subject or raises other issues, don't get sucked in. Say, "We could talk about that later on, but right know I do think we should sort this out." That way, they know you are not dismissing them out of hand, but you are sticking to your purpose.

7 End on a positive note
Once you have explained your problem, suggest that you work out a solution together, "So now you know how embarrassed that made me feel, what do you think we can do to avoid it happening again?"

When you have had your say, and made your feelings clear, always try to leave the other person feeling that the exchange has been positive.

You could say something like, "I feel much better now you have let me tell you how I feel," or, "It's good that we can sort things out and still be friends." This makes your friend feel that they have made a positive contribution to the discussion, rather than just being on the receiving end of your anger.

HOW TO HANDLE THE PUT DOWN

Life being what it is, there will come a time when you are on the receiving end of someone else's anger or criticism. Even the most confident of guys feels pretty miffed when their best mate tells them they have BO, or their gear is naff. When someone runs you down, you feel:

- As if a football has just hit you in the stomach.
- As if you are the world's greatest idiot.
- Unloved.
- Angry.
- A failure.

People respond to criticism in different ways:

Outraged Oliver explodes with fury that anyone should dare to question his judgement or disagree with his actions and storms off in a rage, refusing to listen to a word. Oliver never learns any lessons about himself and so he never makes any changes. He just gets more and more angry because people avoid him.

Silent Selena clams up the moment anyone passes even the slightest criticism. Even when she is being wrongly accused, she bites her lips, folds her arms over her chest and looks miserable. Then she goes home and tells herself she is a social outcast, a friendless failure and doesn't deserve to be happy.

Self-centred Steve listens to criticism, says, "Oh sorry," and does precisely the same thing the following week. Deep down, Steve is only interested in himself and sees the word sorry as a password to bring the conversation to an end, without ever really thinking about what is being said and his part in it.

How do you parry the put down?

Alexander is 15 and was really mortified when his English teacher gave him three bad marks in a row for essays that he had worked on for days. *"The first time I just went home in a mood; the second time I moaned for hours to my best friend but when it happened again, I went to my teacher and told her that I had given the work my best shot and asked what areas I did badly in. She sat down and went through them and in the end decided she had marked me over-harshly and put me up a grade. My term average was better just because I had plucked up the courage to talk about it."*

Dina's problem was her boyfriend's mum. *"She kept making snide comments like, 'You ought to do something with that greasy hair, dear,' and, 'With your type of skin, you can't afford to go without make-up'. It made me really miserable and I began to dread going over to Rick's house. Then one day, I said, 'If I didn't know you better, I would think you were being deliberately unkind.' She looked very sheepish and hasn't said anything nasty for weeks."*

Checklist for taking crits on the chin
• Listen to what is being said.
• Think about it.
• If what they say is true, admit it!
• If they are saying something general like, "You were so stupid!", ask them in what way they mean.
• If you don't really think the issue is important, try a few non-committal comments. "You could be right", "That may be true", or "I can see what you mean".
• If you think you are being criticised unfairly, say so. Don't throw another criticism back; saying, "What do you know about anything?" is childish. Saying, "I honestly don't see how I could have handled that any differently under the circumstances," is much better.

You won't always feel brave enough to be assertive, but when you are, give yourself a pat on the back and enjoy the feeling of standing up for yourself!

Chapter 5

●●●●●●●●●●●●●●●●●●●●●●●●●●●●●●●

SAYING NO

"Don't compromise yourself, you are all you've got."
Janis Joplin, American singer (1943-1970)

"No" is the hardest word in the English language. It may be easy to spell and quick to say – if only you could get it out in the first place and then not spend two days worrying about having said it.

There are many reasons why people worry about saying no.

WHY PEOPLE WORRY ABOUT SAYING NO

1   If I say no, my friend won't like me any more

Everyone wants to be popular and we imagine that if we say no to our friends they won't want us around any more.

Megan is 14 and an only child. Last year she moved to a new town where she knew no one. When the "in" crowd in her year asked her to go to the shopping mall, she was really pleased. The trouble started when a couple of them bought some cans of extra strong cider and dared the rest of them to drink it. *"I knew it was stupid, but I was so grateful that someone at my new school had taken notice of me and I didn't want them thinking I was a wimp. They kept offering me more and I drank three cans. When it made me sick, they all laughed at me anyway. In the end I decided it wasn't worth going round with them because it wasn't making me happy."*

Megan discovered that people who only like you when you fall in with all their plans and agree with every word they say are immature, self-centred and probably only using you.

2 Saying no always ends in trouble

To say no with conviction takes a lot of practice and you don't get a great deal of chance to try it out when you are growing up. When you were four, and yelled, "No – shan't eat my cabbage!" and hurled your plate on the floor, you found yourself banished to your room for an hour for wasting good food. When you were six and your mother told you it was time for bed, you shouted, "No! Shan't! Go away!" and were told that you would do as you were told or else. You weren't quite sure what the "or else" meant and you thought it might be best not to find out.

3 It's so much easier to say yes

Damien is 16 and last year his father lost his job and had to take one which paid a lot less money. Damien's mum went back to work and he took a Saturday job at a local hotel. One day, Damien's mum asked him to fetch some clothes from the dry cleaners and when Damien got there, the manager told him he had found some papers in a trouser pocket. They were betting slips, for large sums of money. Damien confronted his father who made him promise not to tell his mother that he was gambling.

"He said that if I kept quiet, he would split his next big win with me," confessed Damien. "I didn't know what to do. I didn't want to show my dad up, but I couldn't bear to see my mum working all hours, just to have him blow the money on horses. In the end I told her. Now, eight months later, Dad has been given help, the gambling has stopped and next week he has an interview for a job he is really keen on. I am glad I said no when he tried to bribe me to keep quiet."

4 I feel so mean if I say no

Guilt is a major factor in our reluctance to say no. We are all taught that Nice People:

- Think of others before themselves.
- Do unto others as they would wish others to do unto them.
- Think of the common good.

So when we even consider turning down a friend's request, and see the pained expression that crosses their face, we feel very guilty.

Often friends, parents and teachers can be so persuasive: your father will say, "Surely it's not too much to ask you to clean the car tomorrow, is it?" or your friend will say, "If you really cared about me, you would come and do my highlights tonight." Both are implying that if you were *really* nice you would give in to their request and when you say no, you feel bad.

The best way of coping with this is to think of the consequences of saying yes.

- If you give in to your friend, you won't have time to practise for the wind band concert and your homework

will not get handed in on time.
• If you give in to your dad, you will miss the basketball trials and lose the chance of making the team.

5 If I say no, it will look rude and they might not ask me again

To say no in a curt manner with no explanation *is* rude. To say it clearly and concisely and to explain the reason for the refusal is the adult way of handling it. "Thank you for asking me to go swimming but I am tied up all day tomorrow – maybe we could do it next week?" shows the other person that you were pleased by their suggestion and that your reason for refusal has nothing to do with your opinion of them. If it is the swimming you don't fancy, say so. "I'd really enjoy doing something with you this weekend, but I am afraid I'm no water baby."

6 Everyone else is saying yes

Few people enjoy confrontation and sometimes saying yes seems like an easy option. It isn't. If you say yes when you really want to say no people will see through you and think you are wet for not having opinions of your own. You will end up feeling angry for allowing yourself to be manipulated and creating an image of yourself which is not real.

As you grow up, there will be times when you have to say no, not just to your friends, your parents or your teachers, but also to yourself.

HOW TO SAY NO

1 Say the word "No" as early in your reply as you can – if possible, make it the first word of all. "No, I can't come out tonight"; "No, doing that would be really unkind to Sasha"; "No, I don't smoke, thank you."

2 Keep your explanation short. It is much more effective to say, "No, I cannot come and help with your homework tonight because I am tied up," than to say, "Well, I would, only I've got this ballet exam coming up and I need to practise, and I have to deliver my gran's birthday present..." One of the problems with lengthy explanations is that they give your friend the chance to find loopholes – "Well, I'll deliver the present on my way home and then you could come over."

3 Give reasons, not excuses. If the reason you are turning down a request is because you are tired, say so. Don't pretend that you are going out or that your dad's car has broken down and you can't get a lift; you may well be found out and then your refusals will carry no weight next time.

4 Don't keep apologising! It's not a sin to say no. By all means say, "It is a pity I cannot help you out this time," but don't say, "Oh, I am sorry. Really. I am so sorry. Do you hate me? Oh, dear, I feel awful – I am sorry." You are tempting the other person to say, "If you are *that* sorry, why did you say no?"

5 Don't back down. If you say no, and your friend goes off in a huff, don't dash after him and say, "I've changed my mind; I'll do it." He will feel that he has power over you and can force you into situations simply by threatening to turn against you.

6 Don't feel guilty! If you say no to something because it doesn't feel right for you, you have no reason to feel guilty. If you say yes, and go against your own principles, you do have cause for guilt because you have let yourself down.

Taro is 13 and finds that, "Perhaps another time" is a good phrase to add after the initial no. *"It tends to prevent the other person going on at you. But there are some things I would never do and then I say so – like refusing a cigarette by saying that it would be bad for my asthma, or simply admitting that I just don't fancy doing what they do."*

WHEN IT IS HARD TO SAY NO

Saying no to people you don't like, or whose ideas are so contrary to your own that there is no debate, is easy. Saying no to people you love, people whose opinion matters to you, or people to whom you have looked up for a long time, is much, much more difficult. But there are times when it simply has to be done.

Rebecca is 15. *"Last year I started going out with Rajiv who is Indian. We get on really well and have a real laugh together. My dad didn't approve; he said mixed-race friendships only ended in tears. He told me to stop seeing him. I was really upset and talked it all through with my mum. She said that I should explain my feelings clearly to my father. I told him that I knew that it was his house, and I would agree not to bring Rajiv home, but that I didn't really think it was fair for my father to try to choose my friends for me. For a while, things were really difficult; but then my dad met Rajiv's dad at the golf club and now they play together and Rajiv is allowed to come to the house."*

Tim is 14. *"One weekend I was out with a gang of boys from my school and Leigh got this idea of getting some alcoholic lemonade and tipping it into ordinary bottles and giving it to some kids to see what would happen. I knew that it was too strong for little kids and told them not to do it. They told me I was a wimp and that if I didn't go along with the scam, I couldn't go round with them any more. I admit I was tempted to join in, but then I thought about my little sister who is 7 and what would happen if she drank that stuff. So I went home and told my dad."*

SAYING NO TO SEX

If a boy you are really keen on starts pressuring you to go further than you want, it can be really hard to say no. This doesn't just apply to full-blown sex; you have to feel comfortable for any form of intimacy and it is just as difficult to say no to a kiss as it is to refuse to go the whole way.

Sometimes a guy will come up with "reasons" why you should say yes.

1 All my mates sleep with their girlfriends
Don't let this influence you; for one thing, it probably isn't true – lads are Olympic-standard braggers! And even if it is, that is their concern. If it doesn't feel one hundred per cent right for you, don't do it!

Your best reply? "I really like you but I am not ready for that sort of commitment yet."

2 Why not? You're sixteen – it's legal

He has probably been viewing your sixteenth birthday as a key that will open the door to unlimited passion without stopping to think that age has nothing to do with feeling ready for sex.

Your best reply? "Cigarettes are legal but I've no intention of smoking."

3 You've been nice to me all evening – you can't let me down now

If you *have* been coming on really strong, you can't blame the guy for responding. But quite often, this is just his way of explaining away his own arousal. He may say he will suffer agonies if you say no – but he will get over it. Give in, and you may not.

Your best reply? "I've been nice to you because I really like you. Don't let's spoil that."

4 If you really loved me, you would

A tried and tested line which shouldn't carry any weight at all. It simply isn't true – because you love someone, you do not have to compromise yourself.

Your best reply? "If you loved me, you wouldn't put this kind of pressure on me."

5 We've been going out for months and it's time we did it

This is an intimate act we are talking about, not taking a driving test or redecorating a bedroom.

Your best reply? "I wasn't aware this was a

timetabled activity; I will do it if and when I feel happy with it and not before."

One of the things that makes saying no so hard is that you conjure up in your mind a whole array of things that might happen if you do.

But what if...
...he thinks I'm immature?
Saying what you want and what you do not want is a sign of maturity. If he doesn't realise this, then he has a lot of growing up to do and you are better off looking for a guy who respects your decisions.

... he thinks I'm not interested in him?
If he is really keen on you, he is not going to dump you because you say no to sex. If he does, he wasn't worth having in the first place. You can tell him you really fancy him and enjoy being with him but that you are not ready for anything heavy.

...he thinks I'm a tease?
He may accuse you of leading him on, but it is your right to say no at any point in the proceedings that you choose. Remember, however, that if you give out come-on signs on a regular basis and then back off, he may start to question your motives which won't do the relationship any good. Better to have a heart to heart and set your parameters early on.

Girls who just want to have fun!
Don't ever think that it is only boys who put pressure on their girlfriends. Many girls who crave love and

affection can be pretty skilful at implying that a guy is only half a man unless he devotes his entire life to her. Whether she wants you to phone her three times a night, never speak to another girl or make wild passionate love to her and swear undying devotion – if you're not comfortable with it, don't do it. And remember, sex with an underage girl is illegal. Don't listen to, "No one will never find out," "Nothing can go wrong the first time," or "I bet you can't do it."

SO JUST HOW GOOD ARE YOU AT SAYING NO?

1 You are in a large store with your friend and she suggests you pinch some eyeliner pencils from a display. Do you:
a) Say, "No, that's dishonest and I don't want to be involved," and then try to persuade her not to either?
b) Say, "You might be a low-down common thief, but I'm not!"?
c) Do it because you don't want to fall out with her?

2 You are at a party and someone offers you drugs, saying, "They are harmless – no worse than having a shandy." Do you:
a) Say, "No thank you," very firmly and tell your parents what happened?
b) Say, "Only mindless jerks meddle with drugs!"?
c) Take it rather than be thought a killjoy?

3 You are really keen on your boyfriend but he wants to go further than you do. Do you:

a) Say, "No," and then explain why?
b) Say, "Get off me, you pervert!"?
c) Do what he wants, even though you feel uncomfortable, because you are afraid of losing him?

4 You are choosing your exam options and your father is pushing you to take physics. You find science difficult and would much rather study German. Do you:
a) Say, "No Dad, I'm afraid I shall never be an Einstein!"?
b) Say, "It's my life and I'll do what I want"?
c) Sign up for physics to save a row?

5 Your mum's best friend asks you to baby-sit on Saturday but you already have other plans. When you refuse, she says, "Oh dear, you were my last hope. I've got tickets for the theatre and now I'll have to give them away." Do you:
a) Smile and say, "I am going to a party on Saturday – perhaps I could help you out the following week?"?
b) Say, "Tough luck!" and storm off?
c) Say, "OK then, I'll do it," and cancel your date?

6 Your parents have gone away for the weekend to celebrate their Silver Wedding anniversary and told you that you are not to have any parties or sleepovers while they are away. At nine o'clock on Saturday, a gang from school turn up with bottles of beer and suggest you send out for pizzas. Do you:
a) Say, "No, I am not allowed to have parties while my parents are away – we could all go down to Pizza Pie together"?

b) Say, "Well, OK, but don't tell my dad, will you?"?
c) Shut the door firmly and put the chain on – and phone a neighbour at the first sign of trouble?

Answers:
Mostly a's. Good. By saying no at once it leaves no doubt of your reaction and by giving an explanation they can't really complain. If you can make it light-hearted, all the better. Where something might be very dangerous – as in the case of drugs – you must tell someone to prevent a tragedy; that's not sneaking, it's sense.

Mostly b's. You can certainly say no – but you'll probably manage to antagonise whoever you're talking to. Much better to be less aggressive.

Mostly c's. If you got mostly c's then, at best, you never get a chance to do what you want to do, and at worst, you are being very stupid, and sometimes downright dangerous.

Saying no is never easy. It takes practice and sometimes you wish you didn't have to do it. But saying yes when you mean no is much worse and can land you in big trouble.

Chapter 6

• •

OUT WITH IT:
saying what you mean and meaning what you say

*"I tell the truth, not as much as I would but as much as I dare –
and I dare more and more as I grow older."*
Michel de Montaigne, French essayist, (1533-1592)

WHY IT'S IMPORTANT TO SAY WHAT YOU MEAN

Getting people to understand what you are trying to say can be difficult because it is not always easy to say what you really mean. It's easier to let people know when you are happy or excited or proud or grateful, but much harder to let them know when you feel sad or embarrassed or nervous or angry or frightened. Sometimes you only tell half the story or end up pretending that you mean something totally different. And sometimes you decide that it is easier to stay completely quiet and not admit to anything.

This can be for a number of different reasons. You don't want people to think you are silly and you don't want to risk falling out with your friends. Sometimes it is hard to know how to put what you want to say in a way that won't sound unkind and sometimes you know you are going to have to admit you were wrong!

No wonder staying silent seems like the perfect option!

The problem is that your friends don't have a crystal ball. They cannot guess what you really mean. All they have to go on is what you say. So if your best mate starts chatting to you, and you snap, "Oh, just go away and leave me alone!", you cannot blame him if he feels rejected and a bit put out. You know the real reason is that you feel miserable and don't want him to see you in tears – he assumes you have gone off him in a big way. If you say, "I'm feeling pretty awful right now – I'll catch you later," he realises that it is the problem that is bothering you and not him.

It takes a long time to learn how to be honest about what you feel. It's so easy to send out the wrong message and let the words you *say* hide the way you *feel*.

What you say to your teacher: The netball team doesn't stand a hope of winning the tournament.
What you mean: I feel really disappointed at not being selected because I think I could have been a real asset.
What you could say: I had hoped to be Goal Defence; can you tell me what made you leave me out?

What you say to your best friend: I look a real mess, don't I?
What you mean: Please tell me I look all right or I won't feel comfortable going to the disco.
What you could say: I am not sure about this PVC skirt – what do you think?

What you say to your scout master: I can't go on the canoeing trip – my gran is coming to stay.
What you mean: I am terrified of water but I feel ashamed to admit it.

What you could say: Watersports are not my thing but I'd love to come on the hillwalking trip next month.

What you say to a mate: Can't you take a joke?
What you mean: I didn't mean to put my foot in it and I feel guilty for hurting you.
What you could say: I am sorry – that came out all wrong and I didn't mean it to sound like that.

What you say to your mother: I wish you and Dad would shut up.
What you mean: I feel scared that these arguments mean you two are going to split up.
What you could say: I love you both and I am worried about the way you fight. Is everything all right?

In addition to letting people know how you *feel*, you sometimes have to let them know what you *want*. This doesn't mean rushing up to your father as he puts the key in the front door and saying, "I need Nike trainers, £25 for concert tickets and a lift to the bowling alley at 7.22 precisely please." On the other hand, if your friend asks what you want to do at the weekend, and you say, "I don't mind," it is no use complaining when he drags you to watch stock car racing and you really wanted to go to the local soccer Derby.

SPEAKOUT STRATEGIES

When your little sister keeps using your make-up as finger paint and your mum says she's cute:

Don't say: You always did love her best.
Do say: I don't mind playing with her for an hour each evening but I can't have her messing up my things.

When the class bully taunts you because English is your second language and you sometimes get the words wrong:
Don't say: Sorry.
Do say: I know – you speak to me in Bengali on Fridays and I'll work harder at my English the rest of the week.

When your teacher asks if you have understood the principles of velocity and you haven't a clue about any of it:
Don't say: I guess so.
Do say: I still don't understand – could you go over it with me again, please?

When your best friend asks you to go to Laser Quest but you are strapped for cash:
Don't say: I don't fancy it.
Do say: I'd love to but I am totally broke this week. Maybe next time?

If saying how you feel is hard, then telling your friends things you think they would rather not hear is just as difficult. The secret to delivering home truths in a friendly wrapping is to try to make your comments positive, even when their message is negative. If your best mate is trying on a lime green shirt that makes her look as if she has a nasty disease, don't say, "You look awful." Try something like, "That's a great shape, but why not try the lilac one; you look fantastic in that shade".

I HAVE RIGHTS TOO!

Like everyone else, you have the right to:

- State your needs.
- Say you don't understand.
- Change your mind.
- Be treated with respect.
- Make mistakes.
- Express your feelings.
- Set your own goals.
- Express your opinions.
- Decide whether to say yes or no.
- Refuse to take responsibility for other people's problems (this is not the same as refusing to help with other people's problems!).

With those rights come responsibilities. It is no good arguing for your right to be consulted about decisions which affect you if you won't then state clearly what you want. And you can't expect your opinions and feelings to be treated with respect, if you don't listen courteously and sympathetically to other people's viewpoints.

Chapter 7

• •

FRIEND SPEAK

*"I have never wished to cater to the crowd; for what I know,
they do not approve; and what they approve, I do not know."*
Epicurus, Greek philosopher (341-270 B.C.)

Everyone wants to be popular, to feel part of the "in" crowd and to know that there are always people rooting for you and taking your part. When you are not part of a group, or don't have a particular close friend, you start wondering whether there is something wrong with you, some hidden flaw that prevents anyone liking you.

As you grow up, your needs and values change. Little kids are happy to do most things with their families; when you get older, you see a Saturday visit to the garden centre as social death and brain numbing boredom! When they are young, boys want to be tough and brilliant at football; when they get older, being cool is all. Teenage girls want to talk about make-up, and boys and fashion and boys and music and boys! And they want to do it for hours on end without interruption, hesitation or deviation!

WHAT'S GOOD, AND WHAT'S NOT
SO GOOD ABOUT GROUPS

Being part of a group feels good because it allows you to do all the things you want to, while still having a sense of belonging. So it offers a step between that stage of your life when you do almost everything with your family to the time when you go it alone. Different people get different things from being part of a crowd.

Ursula is 13. *"The best bit about being in a group is that you can discuss all sorts of things over and over and it doesn't matter what you say. You can talk about anything; conservation, sex, problems at home and no one tells you that you aren't old enough to have an opinion."*

Russ is 16 and got into his crowd of friends through a common interest. *"I play the drums and my best mate is a blast on the saxophone. We got together with two other guys and formed a band. We played at school concerts and even got asked to take part in a Youth Rock Night for charity. We don't do so much now because of exams, but we still go everywhere together and are really good friends."*

Kirsty is 14. *"The best bit for me about being with a group of friends is that I can ask things that I would never dream of talking about in front of my parents. I only have to mention sex or drugs or working abroad to them and they assume I am going to get pregnant, sniff glue and leave home! With friends, you can explore all the 'What ifs' without anyone getting heavy."*

But there are aspects of being a groupie that are not so good. Sometimes the group you are in may have ideas which you don't share. If they decide that bunking off school is a scam, you may be torn between going along with them in order to remain friends, or doing what you know is right and risking being ridiculed. There may be times when expressing yourself in a group is really difficult, particularly if your views are different from those of the majority or when by following the herd, you risk losing your own identity.

Always remember that you are a unique individual and just because you like going around with a crowd of guys, that doesn't mean you have to imitate them down to the last stick-on tattoo!

WHAT ABOUT WHEN YOU ARE OUT OF THE "IN" CROWD?

When you are feeling down about being an outsider, it helps to stop and think about the phrase "the in crowd". Consider all the fashions that come and go: skirts zip from mini to maxi and back again in the space of three seasons; one year it is hip to wear flatties, the next you have to be seen in four inch wedges; and no sooner have you spent a small fortune on rap and reggae than acid house is back in vogue.

Sometimes it is like that with people. The guy who is the centre of every scam in Year Nine may well be on the sidelines by the time he is in the sixth form.
People are often unpopular for silly reasons at school – for instance because the "in" person doesn't like them, because they're very clever, because they like reading and so are perceived as a swot, because they speak in a different way from everyone else...the list is endless. Even if you are not particularly popular at school, this does not mean that you never will be.

Rosalind is now 31 and a successful playwright. *"When I was at school, I was fat, hopeless at games and much preferred reading to taking part in clubs. When we had to pick teams, I was always the one no one wanted on their side. I used to pretend I didn't care, but it hurt like crazy. I was also very shy and never had a boyfriend, which at my school was social death! I really envied this girl called Erica, who was slim, tall and the most popular girl in the class and had boys lining up to take her out. When I went back to a school reunion last year – having had five plays staged in the West End, and married with adorable two year old twins (and still a size 20!) – I met Erica. She is single, working in a bank and says she is bored brainless. I know it's wicked, but I felt quite smug!"*

Derrick is now 23. *"I admit that I was not at all popular at school – I was a pretty uptight kid, very musical and quite brainy. Coming top of the class all the time sounds great but it doesn't endear you to everyone! I tended to sink myself into work because I always felt left out of the main gangs. But when I went to university I became involved in a music group and we started running workshops for disadvantaged and handicapped children. You really have to put your own inhibitions to one side to do that – and I suddenly found people were turning to me for ideas and saying what a laugh I was! No one was more surprised, or happier, than me!"*

WHAT MAKES SOMEONE POPULAR?

There is a myth that says that if someone is popular, they are automatically going to be an ace friend for all time. That isn't necessarily so. True, many of the attributes that make a good friend, like being kind, having a sense of humour, responding to the needs of others – can often been found in the most popular people in school. But some popular people can be quite intimidating especially to those who are not part of their immediate circle; others are popular only because of something they can do or offer, and not because of lasting qualities in themselves. So if you are not kingpin of your class it doesn't mean that you are not worth knowing or fun to be with.

So just what is it that makes someone popular?

1 Being mature

Most people growing up aspire to be adult as quickly as possible. Everyone gets there, but they do it at different speeds and sometimes the girl who has got past the flat chested, spotty and nervous stage, has sussed which clothes look good on her and can give you the low-down on everything from which mascara won't run to the best cure for period pains, becomes the centre of attention. This isn't because she is any nicer, funnier, cleverer or more sincere that you are; simply because sub-consciously people hope that one day – preferably very soon – they will be as together as she is.

2 Being confident

People who don't mind saying what they think, standing up for what they believe is right and challenging issues that confront them are often hugely popular. These are the guys people turn to when a problem needs solving – the ones who have the courage to question the Head on the new school rule, or stand up to the class bully. A confident person makes those around him feel secure and so they gravitate towards spending more and more time in his company.

3 Being sporty

It is a sad fact for those of us who cannot run without falling over our own feet, and whose ball control is non-existent, that being good at sport is a great boost along the road to popularity, especially for boys. But if you are one of those who take no joy from spending a nose-numbing hour on a half-frozen rugby pitch, take heart. The type of popularity afforded to the captain of soccer or the school's Bowler of the Year comes largely from the corporate urge to win, to take the team to glory and to be better than the opposition. If the boy in question can't back up his sporting prowess with some pretty likeable qualities off the field, his popularity will be as transient as England's success on the cricket circuit.

4 Being cool

People who are easy to talk to, who don't flap or make snap judgements and who are sufficiently in tune with what's hip and hot are fun to be with – and not hard work! That's why they are popular.

5 Being attractive

This is something everyone can be, because it doesn't mean that you have to have a supermodel figure, flawless skin and symmetrical teeth. It doesn't require you to have the physique of a body builder or the looks of a film star. All that being "attractive" means is that you have qualities that will attract others to you – a ready smile, a sense of fun, an ability to shut up and listen to what other people are saying and a willingness to help out. And that is something everyone can cultivate!

6 Being enthusiastic

People who repeatedly say things like, "There's no point", "It's a waste of time," or, "I can't be bothered," are rarely popular. Those who enter heart and soul into whatever is going on and who don't mind making a fool of themselves occasionally have the kind of infectious good nature that makes other people want to join them.

Sometimes people enjoy a short spell of popularity for very superficial reasons – their dad has just had a swimming pool put in the back garden and everyone wants to be the first to get an invitation; their brother is roadie for Mud Unlimited and everyone reckons they can get freebie tickets; or they have mastered the latest craze and are handing out tips to the less initiated. This kind of popularity doesn't last long and means very little because it is based not on the qualities of the person, but on what they have to offer materially.

SIX WAYS TO ENSURE YOU ARE UNPOPULAR

1 Follow in the footsteps of Aggressive Alan – snap the head off of anyone who fails to agree with your point of view, insist on your needs being met before anyone else's and growl at anyone who gets more attention than you.

2 Copy Self-centred Sarah – who is only happy when she is talking about herself, or persuading others to do things her way. Sarah only gets involved in activities that are of direct benefit to herself and when she finds people are not terribly interested, she has a fit of the sulks (having first made sure everyone is watching).

3 Imitate Killjoy Kevin whose catchphrases are, "It won't work out," "You'll never manage it," and "It's bound to all go wrong." Well, would you hang around for long?

4 Be like Telltale Trish. She promises faithfully to keep a secret and then spills the beans to the entire Year group; she grasses up her friends and talks about other people behind their backs. And when she discovers that she is all alone, she runs to teacher and says that everyone is being horrid to her.

5 Give orders like Bossy Belinda. She always knows that her way of doing things is the best way and unless she can be in charge of everything and everyone, she doesn't want to know.

6 Complain all the time like Moaning Melissa. If the gang go ice skating, Melissa's too cold; if they check out the new Fun Pool, Melissa doesn't want to get her hair wet. When everyone wants a quiet night in, Melissa moans that they never do anything exciting, but when someone throws a spur-of-the-moment party, it's Melissa who complains that she hasn't anything to wear.

The best way to get high in the popularity ratings is to work out what you like in a friend – and then try to live up to it yourself!

GOSSIP

It's great, isn't it? You curl up with the phone in one hand, a giant bag of Wondercrunch Barbecued Ox crisps in the other and have a good gossip. And for as long as the talk is about whether Dieter Brummer is sexier than Johnny Depp, or that you reckon Karl fancies Cindy and Todd is going to ask Sarah to the ball game, that's fine. But sometimes gossip can get out of hand.

Imagine this. Your friend Dee tells you Holly said that Jane kissed your boyfriend Ben. Now you didn't hear Holly say it; you only heard Dee reporting that Holly had said it. So you confront Holly and say, "Did you say that Jane kissed Ben?"

And she replies, "I didn't say that Jane kissed Ben." So you are happy. Or are you?

It depends how she said it.

I didn't say Jane kissed Ben (but someone else did).

I *didn't* say Jane kissed Ben (I definitely didn't).

I didn't *say* Jane kissed Ben (but I implied it).

I didn't say *Jane* kissed Ben (but someone else kissed him).

I didn't say Jane *kissed* Ben (she did something else with him).

I didn't say Jane kissed *Ben* (she kissed someone else).

Because you can now hear how Holly is imparting this information you can judge what lies behind her words. But when you listen to gossip you don't have that information and sometimes can form quite the wrong opinion.

Tracy nearly lost her good friend Aileen because of gossip. *"Someone told me that Aileen thought I was a totally sad person,"* she said. *"I'm not very trendy and I felt really upset and started ignoring Aileen. After a week, she asked me what on earth she had done and why I was being so off-hand with her. I told her what I had heard and it turned out that she had told this girl I was sad – because my dad had lost his job."*

Remember that people tend to see something and interpret it the way they want; or hear one snippet of conversation and add the remaining details themselves.

"Dave's dad has bought this huge house – they're rolling in money."	Dave's dad has bought a rundown house and got a mortgage and a grant to do it up.
"Kelly's mum is up in court today – she could go to prison."	Kelly's mum is a witness in a road traffic accident case.
"I saw Paul with this stunning girl – so I thought you should know he is two-timing you."	Paul was out with his cousin for the day.

"Luke – I thought you ought to know – Lynn doesn't want to go out with you any more."	Lynn mentioned that she would not be able to see Luke for a week because her dad had grounded her.

If you hear something that bothers you – find out the truth before hitting the ceiling. It saves a lot of energy, a load of heartache – and stops you making a fool of yourself!

YOUR BAD NEWS, MY BAD NEWS: a friend in need is a friend indeed

At some time in everyone's life they have to face issues or events which are unfamiliar and often frightening. Coping with the emotional effects of family illness, parental divorce or even bereavement is difficult at any age but when you are growing up and facing all sorts of other changes as well, you can feel not only confused but lonely.

It is at times like these that friends mean so much. But talking about things that make you sad, or knowing what to say to a friend who is grieving, is not easy. Sometimes you feel that it is simpler just to keep away from everyone for a bit, rather than risk bursting into tears; or to avoid your friend because you don't know how to talk about her dad's death. But remember that your friends want to help, even if they don't know how, and saying anything that is kind and understanding is better than letting your friend imagine she is facing her crisis all on her own.

When Jennifer's father died suddenly from a heart attack, she found that none of her friends really wanted to talk about it. *"They would say they were sorry to hear my news, and then abruptly change the subject. I wanted to talk about Dad and they seemed really anxious. In the end I said, 'It's OK, I find it a real help to talk about the things we used to do together,' and when they saw I wasn't skirting the subject, things were much easier."*

Joshua was grief stricken when his grandmother died. *"What hurt the most was that my best mate Kenneth said, 'Well, she was old, wasn't she?' as if that made it all right. My gran had virtually brought me up till I was nine and I couldn't imagine life without her. I found myself getting really mad at Kenneth because he couldn't understand how I was feeling."*

It is not only friends who find things difficult to talk about. Sometimes your own family feel that it is best to avoid the painful subject.

Sonia's little sister was killed by a hit and run driver when she was eight and Sonia was 12. *"For a long time, I found it so hard to talk to anyone about it. My parents were devastated but they never talked about Kirsty in front of me. Instead, they seemed to get more strict with me and I began to think they wished it was me that was dead and not Kirsty. Whenever I tried to talk to Mum, she cried and changed the subject and for months afterwards, Dad wouldn't let me go anywhere or do anything with my friends. I felt like I had lost them as well as Kirsty. One day I burst into tears at school and ended up telling my teacher how I felt. She saw Mum and Dad and we had a long talk. It turned out that Dad was so afraid that I would have an accident that he wanted to keep me at home and Mum was afraid that I blamed her for Kirsty's death, because she had been at work when it happened. Once we had cleared the air, we all starting talking and now we can laugh about the funny things Kirsty did as well as grieve over her."*

There are some problems that families face which bring out all the prejudice in other people. Phil was 15 when his father was admitted to a psychiatric hospital suffering from a serious mental illness. Phil felt very confused; he had watched his dad changing from the man he had known for years into a withdrawn stranger and was worried about his mother who was taking it very badly. Phil felt he had to be strong for her sake and didn't mention his dad to any of his friends.

But eventually the news got out and two boys in his year began taunting him, calling his father a nutcase and asking if it was hereditary.

"I used to dread going to school until one day a guy I hardly knew from Year Ten heard these two boys saying that my dad was in the funny farm and I was going loopy too. He sent them packing and then told me that his mother had been mentally ill three years before and was now completely recovered. After that, I talked to him a lot and it made such a difference not to have to pretend. The two boys never said anything more about it."

How to say you care

1 You don't have to launch into a long speech – simply saying, "I am sorry to hear about your mum – if you want to talk, you know I am always ready to listen," is the greatest gift you can offer your grieving friend.

2 When something bad has happened, people often

feel defensive. They need to know that you are not blaming them for someone else's actions. Say, "You must be missing your dad so much while he is in prison – if you feel like coming round one evening, it would be great to see you, " or, "I know you must be worrying about your brother but I've heard that drug rehab programme is brilliant."

3 If you cannot think what to say, buy a little gift – a cuddly bear, a bunch of flowers – and attach a note. Showing you care is the most important thing.

4 Remember that friends often worry that they will lose you if their circumstances change. Reassure them that even if their dad has lost his job and their allowance is cut, you still want to hang out with them on Saturdays. Offer the odd treat – or simply gear your evening to the cheap things.

5 There is no shame in admitting that you don't have the right words. To say, "I wish I could find the words to tell you how sorry I am," is much better than saying nothing at all.

Most of all, be there. Don't be afraid to be the one to say something, anything, to show you care. That is what real friendship is all about.

HOW KIND!:
giving and receiving compliments

Everyone wants to be recognised. That is not to say everyone wants to be famous, to have their face on the cover of *Vogue* or front a chat show on national television. But we all need to feel appreciated and important and we all like a few words of praise.

Considering this, it is strange that we are often reluctant to offer compliments to others and even more ungracious about receiving them ourselves.

Paying a genuine compliment increases a person's sense of self worth; but overdo it, and it loses all its impact and sounds sycophantic.

Compliment – or crawling?
There is a difference between paying someone a genuine compliment and crawling or grovelling.

• You played the piano beautifully in assembly. (compliment)
• You are such a good pianist, but then, you are good at most things – and I don't suppose, I mean being as I am useless at music, could you help me? (crawling)
• That colour really suits you. (compliment)
• I wish I had your sense of style; I could never look like that – you are amazing, honestly you are. (crawling)
• I couldn't have done without your help last night – thank you so much. (compliment)
• I don't know where I would have been without you, what with me being so stupid and getting lost and then not having money for the phone – but then, you would

never do a silly thing like that, would you? (crawling)

Tessa's terrific – pass it on!

There is a saying that bad news travels fast – and often, we are bursting with eagerness to pass on the latest piece of gossip or scandal, but not nearly so quick to repeat the good things we hear about a friend.

Casey used to worry a great deal about letting the swimming team down. *"I only got to swim as reserve when someone else was off sick and I never gained a first place. It wasn't until my friend Vicki told me that the coach had said that steady swimmers like me were the backbone of the relay team that I felt I was contributing something worthwhile."*

Taro is 13, loves acting and rarely suffers from stage fright. *"When someone told me that they had really enjoyed my performance, I was really pleased. It was the first time anyone had actually told me that – I think that because I seem confident, no one thought that I would need to know that I was doing a good job."*

Most of us are only too eager to tell our friends when they overstep the mark or do something we find offensive or upsetting. It's very easy in the middle of a bust-up to run through a list of all their faults and failings. But after the row is over, the tears shed, the making up completed, and you are sitting over a large chocolate milk shake sighing with relief that you are friends again, it is a very good idea to counter all those nasty things you said with a couple of considered compliments. "I'm so glad we've sorted that – what would I do without you to make me laugh?" or, "You are such a good listener – even when I am going way over the top!" That way, your friend knows that she matters and that any differences between you can't shake the solid friendship.

Saying thank you – nicely!

When someone pays you a compliment, they are giving you a gift. If someone gave you a large box of handmade chocolates and you threw it back in their face, you wouldn't be surprised if they were upset. It's the same with compliments. But often, it is more difficult to be gracious about receiving them.

If you don't have a good self image and someone says, "Your new hair style is really flattering," you may well say, "This haystack? I can't do a thing with it," rather than give a broad smile and say, "Thank you very much."

Your teacher says: That essay was a great improvement – well done.
Don't say: It still wasn't as good as Barbara's.
Do say: Thank you – I did try hard.

Your friend says: That goal you scored gave us the match – well done.
Don't say: Just luck.
Do say: Thank you – I am so pleased we won.

Your new boyfriend says: You have the most wonderful eyes.
Don't say: But I've got awful freckles and fat ankles.
Do say: Thank you very much – what a nice thing to say!

Just as giving compliments bolsters your friends' self image, receiving them graciously gives you a kick too!

Chapter 8

••••••••••••••••••••••••••••••

PROBLEM FRIENDSHIP:
when bosom buddiness turns into mate hate

"Instead of loving your enemies, treat your friends a little better."
Ed Howe, American journalist (1853-1937)

Friendships never stand still. They either grow and flourish, or they falter and die. People are changing all the time – because of their age, their circumstances and their experiences – and so it follows that the relationships will also change. If those changes are acceptable, that's fine; but if not, you need to feel able to speak out about the things that bother you and that's not always easy.

Sometimes a friendship runs into difficulties, not because you are both changing, but because one of you has set ideas of what the other "owes" them.

FRIENDS WHO IMPOSE

It is great to have friends who enjoy your company and who want to include you in their plans. But sometimes, especially if you have been eager to be wanted and therefore made yourself readily available, you start to feel as if a particular friend is imposing on you.

Rowena's best friend, Amy, started taking her for granted. *"She would call round at my house unannounced and if I said I was going out, she'd say, 'That's fine; I'll come along too.' Once she signed me up for a school trip without even asking if I wanted to go and when I said it wasn't my scene, she said that I had spoiled it all for her. And she expected me to spend every weekend doing things with her. It was like she felt she owned me."*

Speaking your mind to people like this is not easy. Part of you is worried that if you stand up for yourself and your privacy, you will lose this friend completely; you fear they might tell your other friends that you have let them down and then they will start to think badly of you; and yet another part of you knows that you have neither the time nor the energy to take responsibility for someone else's problems. This is when you have to take a deep breath and say, "No, not this time."

Olivia had to handle a similar situation with her friend Elaine. *"We had been friends for about a year at school and then Elaine's family moved to the same road as me. Elaine started coming round every evening to borrow text books or copy my homework. Her mum just assumed that Elaine could have tea at our house if the rest of her family were out, and my mum got a bit annoyed about it. Although I really liked her, I was just seeing too much of her and not enough of my other mates. I didn't want the friendship to end so one day I told her that I thought we should have set times for seeing each other when we could go out and have fun and not spend the time indoors. We agreed on Saturday afternoons and Tuesday evenings and it's worked really well. Now when I see her I really enjoy her company."*

POSSESSIVE FRIENDS

These are the friends who want you all to themselves, who cannot bear to see you going off bowling with another crowd and who expect to be in on every aspect of your life. To start with, if you haven't had many friends, it feels great to be that important in someone's life and you are only too happy to spend every free moment in their company. But as you gain confidence and meet more people, you find that your horizons are expanding – and your friend resents it.

Lindsay found it really hard to handle when her friend Bianca started joining every club that Lindsay joined. *"At our new school we were encouraged to join activities as a way of getting involved, and I signed up for badminton, the dance and drama group and the cycling club. Two days later, I found Bianca had done the same. It was crazy because she isn't into acting. Art and design is her thing, yet she wouldn't join the craft club because I wasn't a member. She insisted on sitting next to me, doing what I did, and even got upset when I signed up for a cycle trip that her mum had said no to. From really liking her company, I started finding it was all getting too claustrophobic."*

People like Bianca often hang on to their friends like limpets, because they don't have enough confidence in themselves. They prefer to be a shadow to their best friend rather than stand in the sunshine. Lindsay solved the problem quite cleverly. *"When the drama club produced a play, Bianca was miffed because she didn't have a part. I said casually that it was a great shame she wasn't in the craft club because they were making loads of the props. She joined – and now she has two more friends and we are good mates without me feeling like I'm suffocating."*

JEALOUS FRIENDS

When things go well, everyone hopes that their friends will share their delight. They will be ecstatic for you when you win the talent contest or land the lead in the school play. They will enthuse over your Ibiza holiday pictures, giggle as you try to get to grips with the computer your dad bought for your birthday and drop everything to go with you to the mall to spend the wads of cash Granny sent because you passed your exams.

Sometimes it doesn't happen. Instead, they turn green with envy and start making snide remarks.

• You tell them about your forthcoming trip to America and they say, "It's all right for some – my family can only afford a week in Newquay."
• You win the form prize for art and they say, "Well, the competition wasn't that hot this year, was it?"
• At a friend's birthday party, this cool dude asks you to dance but ignores your friend. She spends the rest of the evening telling you everything that is wrong with him and offering you a dozen reasons why you should have nothing to do with him.

Try to remember that most people who show this type of jealousy are feeling very vulnerable and insecure themselves. If you have something they desperately would like, or you have achieved something which makes them feel they are less worthwhile than you, don't go on about it in front of them. Make a point of saying something positive about them. But also, don't let their envy get to you. If you dismiss their retorts with a friendly smile and a non-committal remark, they will see that nothing they say will affect your actions.

And when you feel jealous of a friend, try admitting it. Speaking out is not just about saying what you want, it's about admitting to the painful bits too. John found out that it actually helps.

"When my best mate Leo was invited to spend two weeks with his girlfriend's family in France, I was really churned up about it. He could sense something was wrong and I admitted that I was green with envy. He couldn't see why because my dad was taking me to Portugal a month later. The funny thing was, as we talked about it, I realised I wasn't jealous of the holiday but of the fact that his girlfriend's parents accepted him. My girlfriend's mum thinks we are too young to be going out together. It really helped me see why I felt like I did."

FAIR WEATHER FRIENDS

Just as jealous friends find it hard to cope with your good times, fair weather friends disappear like corn before a locust swarm when the going gets tough. The guy who was happy to call round twice a week when you lived in the big house with the swimming pool is conspicuous by his absence when your dad loses his job and you move to a flat in town. The girl who hung around like a limpet when your sister was working for Random Records and giving you freebie CDs doesn't want to know when the supply of goodies dries up. Fair weather friends frankly are not worth wasting tears over; if they want you for what they can get out of you, and not for yourself, forget them.

"FRIENDS" YOU DON'T KNOW

We've all been there. Your dad comes home and says that his boss's son is starting at your school and he just knows you will be great mates. Your mum makes friends with a woman at her oil painting class and they decide it would be jolly if you got together with her daughter. Suddenly you find yourself thrown at someone you didn't choose, whose interests you don't share and who probably is about as eager to be with you as you are to be foisted on her.

Don't dismiss these people out of hand just because you have been thrown together by your parents – at least until you know for sure that you won't hit it off. It may be that while your dad wants you to befriend the boss's son because it all helps towards good office relations, you will discover that the two of you do have something in common. But if not, don't let anyone else try to keep the friendship going for their own ends. Keeping the friendships you *do* want in good repair is hard enough without trying to keep other people happy.

SURPLUS TO REQUIREMENTS

At some time someone you want to stay friends with won't want to stay friends with you, and you will be dropped. It isn't nice, it isn't comfortable, but the chances are it will happen. And when it does, you will feel miserable, hurt and possibly angry. It happened to Stephanie.

"Michelle, Tracy and I always did everything together but

after a while, I began to sense an atmosphere. I would walk up to the other two and they would stop what they were saying and giggle. Or I would find Tracy had been round to Michelle's house at the weekend and they hadn't included me. Then one day I was in the loo and heard them talking to another girl in the washroom. Tracy said, 'Michelle and I are trying to dump Stephanie – she is just so immature!' I felt really devastated. I felt like I was a failure and it took me weeks to get over it."

It is tempting to blame yourself for being dumped. You think that you must be a horrid person, you worry about whether it was something you said or some gaffe you made that caused the split. And then you start feeling angry and asking yourself how anyone could be so mean as to treat you like that. Anger is a natural reaction to the feeling of rejection but it is important not to let it take over.

What not to do	*What to do*
Cry whenever you see them.	Smile and say, "Hi – how you doing?"
Tell everyone else how much you hate them.	Say, "We used to be really close and it was great but things move on."
Hang around them and beg them to take you back.	Be friendly to other people and make new relationships.
Tell yourself you are horrible and worthless.	Realise that, although they don't want your friendship, others do.

Try to "buy" them back with presents.	Make friends who like you for yourself.

WHEN IT ISN'T WORKING ANY MORE

Some friendships start when people are in nursery school and carry on until they are comparing photographs of their grandchildren. Others are intense for a couple of years and then begin to wane as you develop new interests or meet new friends. And sometimes you simply stop finding pleasure in the company of the mate you used to pine for between Sunday night and Monday morning!

Handling a friendships that isn't working any more requires kindness and tact. It is worth asking yourself why you don't want to be friends any longer.

Good reasons	*Bad reasons*
You have little in common these days.	She won't cover up for you when you miss class.
She's let you down once too often.	She's friends with one guy you think is the absolute pits.
She's been spreading untrue stories about you.	She's never got any money to go out.

If you really do want to stop a friendship, let it happen gradually. Don't pick up the phone one evening and say, "I've decided we've nothing in common so I won't be coming round any more." If you have been seeing one another twice a week, cut it down to once, and then perhaps miss a week, explaining that you have judo class or that you are getting involved with the drama group.

If you are hurt by the way she has behaved, tell her so and say that you think for the time being it might be a good idea to see less of one another. At the same time, tactfully point her in the direction of other people whose company she enjoys. The top tip is to think what you would feel like in her shoes and be as kind as you can.

TOP TIPS FOR SAYING GOODBYE TO YOUR BOYFRIEND/GIRLFRIEND

1 Never be unkind. Saying, "You are boring, babyish and a waste of space," is cruel and indefensible; saying, "We don't seem to have that much in common any more – but I'll always be glad we were friends," leaves the other person feeling valued.

2 Never dump in public. It is hard enough handling rejection without having to cope with the reaction of other people.

3 Never cast blame. If you are dumping a girlfriend, don't say, "It's your fault this didn't work out – you are so self-centred." Simply say that you don't think the relationship is going anywhere and that you think it is better that you are both free to make new friends.

4 Never dump in the middle of an argument. It's very easy to shout, "That's it – I never want to speak to you again!" – and then wake up the following morning wishing you could take it all back. Friendship is precious; think carefully about what you want to say before you open your mouth.

Chapter 9

● ●

PARENT SPEAK

"Go directly; see what she's doing and tell her she mustn't."
(From Punch, 1872)

Teenagers and parents argue. It is a fact of life, like summer following spring and the stores always being out of your size when you have finally managed to save up the cash for that cropped jacket.

Your mother protests, "You don't talk to me any more." Your father complains, "Is that grunt supposed to be an answer – a gorilla in the jungle makes more sense than you!" Your mum says, "You're not old enough to stay out late/go camping with friends/wear that much make-up." Your father says, "When I was your age, I wouldn't have dared answer back like that!"

It's not that you don't want to talk to your parents – about some things, at least! But you want to do it in your time scale and in your way. You are no longer a little kid who rushes home from school to give your mum a minute-by-minute account of your day. You want to release information when you feel like it, and not because someone else demands it. This is why that perennial favourite of all parents – "How was school?" so often elicits a sarcastic reply – "Red brick and in the same place as yesterday."

You want your parents to see you as someone who is ready to take control of their own life. But if you lose your cool, slam doors, throw a fit of the sulks or simply clam up and refuse to speak, they will assume, not without justification, that you are still a kid.

WHAT TEENAGERS AND PARENTS ARGUE OVER

Teenagers argue with parents over a whole range of issues.

• Appearance – their idea of what is "smart" usually conflicts with your idea of what is hip. It helps to save your most funky outfits for socialising with friends and to meet your parents halfway when it's Granddad's 80th birthday!
• Money – you think they should give you more and they know that you have to learn to budget and manage on what you have.
• Curfew rules – they want you in at ten and you know that nothing gets hot till 11. They are thinking of your safety; you are thinking of your street cred!
• House rules – parents love tidy bedrooms, pristine bathrooms, kids who wash up, and music played softly. You can't see what is so important about a vacuumed carpet or gleaming bath.
• Friends – they either think you spend too much time with your mates, or that they are not the ones they would choose. To you, your friends are the most important part of your world and you won't hear a word against them.

• School work – they get so excited over good grades you would think they had done the work themselves. Bad grades cause all manner of hand wringing and accusations of putting boys before biology and parties before physics.

• Boyfriends and girlfriends – viewed with suspicion by parents not only because of the "s" word but because they provide visible proof that their little girl/boy isn't any more.

• Most families have at least a few rules – and those that don't are the unlucky ones. Guidelines are essential when people are living under the same roof – it is just that what your parents see as perfectly sensible, manageable rules seem to you to be cruel constraints on your personal freedom! So you question them. No harm in that. It's the way you question them that matters.

THE ART OF COMMUNICATING WITH THEM

Your parents may have opinions widely different from your own. "So what?" you might think. "I don't have to agree with them." Of course you don't. It's how you disagree that matters.

Remember that parents will go on caring and being concerned about you long after their need to control you has passed. One way you can show them that you are becoming a responsible adult is to show them that you understand how they feel.

What they say: It's 10.30 in the morning and you are still in bed. Get moving, you lazy lump!

Why they say it: Because they recall that good parents ensure their kids eat regularly, get fresh air and do things!

What you say: What's your problem? I'm not hurting anyone.

A better way: I know it's late, but I'm shattered after all those exams and I needed to catch up on some sleep. I'll be down in half an hour.

What they say: What do you see in the guy – nose studs and tattoos! What a scruff!

Why they say it: Because they associate the grunge look with drop outs and ne'er do wells, and don't see it as a fashion statement as valid as pinstripes and a co-ordinating tie.

What you say: It's not up to you to choose my friends.

A better way: I know you don't like that style of dressing, Dad, but Todd's a great guy and really good to me, and I want to go on seeing him.

What they say: Camping in Devon with your friends? At 15? No way.

Why they say it: They love you, are worried sick about your safety, know that you are growing up, know they have to face your freedom and want to put it off as long as possible.

What you say: Everyone else's parents are cool about it – why do you have to be so possessive?

A better way: Look, this is the name of the campsite – and here's the phone number. Darren's mum is going to drive us up there – why don't you give her a call and talk about it?

Just as kids do things and want things that annoy and worry their parents, so parents can behave in ways that their children find either irritating or embarrassing. For Juliet, who is 14, it is her mum's behaviour in front of her friends.

"I just can't stand it when my mum starts asking my friends questions when they come over to the house – like she is trying to be sugary sweet and friendly. It drives me mad. And one time she was driving me and a mate to the disco and we were singing this song and she joined in. I thought I would die. Later, I told her never to humiliate me like that again, and she blew her top and we had the most awful row."

With Ian, it's his dad. *"Dad is such a know-all. No matter what my friends and I are talking about, he interrupts and sets us straight. When I told him how irritating it was, he simply said, 'I've been around longer than you.' It snowballed into this dreadful argument and we ended up shouting names at each other."*

Arguments and outbursts leave everyone feeling screwed up and miserable. But if you are clever you can at least work things so that your parents will give you a fair hearing.

1 Ask them what things were like when they were your age. What did they argue about with their own parents? (If they say nothing, don't believe them.) Say something like, "Did you fight with Gran about staying out late?" or, "I bet your dad flipped when you wore those mini skirts and plastic boots?" Then go on to ask how they handled their parents and whether they think they were fair. This is a very clever approach because people love talking about themselves and most people want to make a better job at being parents than their own parents did.

2 Give them a chance to express their point of view. If you ask why you cannot do something and they say, "Because we say so!", don't lose your rag. Say, "Is it that you are worried for my safety, or do you think we can't afford the cost?" That way, you put them in a position where they have to consider their own reasons and give you an answer. Once they have told you what is bothering them, you can discuss it rationally.

3 If you really have a hard time getting a hearing, it is sometimes a good idea to invite one of your friends whom your parents really like to come round to the house. Then steer the conversation to the topic of dispute. You could say something like, "I was hoping to go to the Jazz Fest with you on Saturday, but Mum doesn't like the idea, do you, Mum?" Don't expect her to change her mind necessarily; but she will want to appear reasonable in front of your friend, and will be much less likely to lose her rag.

4 Be prepared to compromise. If your parents say you have to be in by 10.30 and you want to stay out till midnight, try to settle for 11 o'clock. Neither side have won hands down, but no one has totally lost either.

When the going gets tough
If discussing curfews and cash flow crises is tricky, handling really serious problems is even harder.

If you are in serious trouble, it is difficult to pluck up the courage or to find the right words. And if you don't get on with them all that well in the first place, you are probably going to be really worried about telling them something difficult – such as the fact that you have been suspended from school, have been caught shop lifting or are pregnant.

Nothing is going to make it easy – but putting it off will certainly make it harder, so do it as soon as you can.

• Try to choose a time when they are not pre-occupied. If they are dashing around grabbing briefcases and making phone calls before hurtling to the office, they won't want to stop.
• If they seem reluctant to stop what they are doing and give you their undivided attention, say, "I really do need to talk to you very soon about something important." If they still show no signs of paying attention, insist that you all agree a time when they will be free.
• Don't dither. Take a deep breath and say, "I have a very real problem and I need your help and support in dealing with it." Be prepared for their reaction; it may be anger, distress, panic, fear or just stunned silence. Allow them to take in what you have told them before you take the discussion further.
• Take responsibility: "I know I did wrong by taking alcohol into school and I deserve the suspension."
• Don't be afraid to admit how you feel. There is no shame in saying, "I am so ashamed of what I did and feel I cannot face anyone," or, "I've been feeling so depressed that I just want to lock myself in my room and sleep." And don't be afraid to cry. It relieves your feelings and shows your parents how you feel.

Sometimes they may not realise that you are unhappy, and assume that you are just in a mood.

Talking to your parents can be a drag. Not talking to them can build barriers which take years to knock down. You may not always manage what the politicians call a "full and frank exchange of views" but at least talking is better than living side by side in stony silence!

HOW TO COPE WHEN YOUR PARENTS DON'T LIKE YOUR FRIENDS

Most parents like to get to know their children's friends. They say things like, "When are we going to meet this Samantha who seems to have the answers to all the world's problems?" and, "If Jon is such a great guy, how come we've never seen him?"

You may feel resentful about their insistence on casting an eye over your friends; after all, how often do you demand to vet their dinner party guest list? On the other hand, it is reassuring to know that they care enough abut you to want to meet your friends and know who it is you are going around with, and who ties up their telephone lines for three hours every night.

More often than not, you bring your friends home and after the obligatory ten minutes of polite chat over a digestive biscuit, your mother gets bored and goes off to water her petunias and you can relax. Occasionally, however, you are faced with:

The post mortem
This usually begins with something along the lines of:

"Couldn't you find someone a bit more like us?"

"I didn't think much of his manners."

"How could her mother let her out looking like that?"

Shortly followed by:

"Whatever happened to that nice Angela you went to ballet with?"

Tempting as it is to tell your mother that nice Angela turned out to be a two-faced little sneak with the loyalty quotient of a preying mantis, and that you choose your friends, not for their skill with a knife and fork, but for their fun factor – desist. Such retorts only induce soaring parental blood pressure, long-winded accounts of how you don't know you're born and a determination to view this new friend with suspicion from hereon in.

Instead, when they ask – and they will – what you see in him or her, be honest. Tell them that your friend makes you laugh, shares the same interests or is easy to talk to.

And then, with a smile and very charmingly, ask them what they have against this friend, and why.

What they may say: She's a bad influence.

What they probably mean: She's different from us and we are scared.

Why? Parents of teenagers get scared; it comes with the job, like always having enough pizza in the freezer to feed five thousand and giving up Saturday nights to ferry you round the county. They worry that your friend might encourage you to take drugs, bunk school, drop your grades, waste your life...and so on.

What they may say: You spend too much time in idle chat.
What they probably mean: We're jealous.
Why? After a decade of your total devotion, they now discover that what Rebecca says is more important than what Mum says, and if Dave approves, then Dad's opinions can go hang. They know this is a normal part of your development but that doesn't make it any easier to cope with.

What they may say: He thinks too much of himself.
What they probably mean: We feel old.
Why? When your dad hears Warren talking about setting off on Operation Raleigh or Pippa tells your mum that she intends to be fashion editor of *Elle* by the time she is 28, the parental memories go whizzing back to the days when they thought they could conquer the universe. Suddenly they feel old and past it, and when they say, "She thinks she is God's gift to creation," they really mean, "I wish I was that young and enthusiastic again."

What they may say: They are not our type.
What they probably mean: We don't understand them and that is scary.
Why? Everyone's scared by the unknown. So whether your friend is from a different religion, different culture or even just speaks with a different accent, you parents may worry that your new friend will encourage you to reject all the values they have tried to instil in you or that you will discover new ways of living which will exclude them.

By understanding the hidden meaning behind their words, you are in control. There is no need to respond with hasty remarks like, "That shows how little you know," and, "You are so bigoted." Rather than criticise their feelings, acknowledge them.

If they are worried about your going astray, reassure them. "There is no way Jackie is into that kind of scene, and if she was, I certainly wouldn't follow."

If you guess they feel as if they are being ignored, explain. "You've always told me that people learn by exchanging views – and that's what I enjoy about being with Tony."

If you think they feel old and past it, reassure them. "I was telling Warren about the time you and Dad cycled round the Hebrides – he thinks you're brilliant. Come to think of it, you two should take it up again – it would be great."

If you suspect they are worried about you mixing with people of a different creed and culture, acknowledge this. "Marie is a really kind person – and her family know I'm vegetarian and they never serve meat when I'm invited round."

When things go wrong

Things won't always go swimmingly, no matter how hard you try. There may be times when your parents are proved right; perhaps your grades do crash because you and your friend have spent too much time playing computer games and not enough completing assignments. Maybe you go to a party and in the excitement drink too much and get sick. Your parents may well blame your friend's influence – but you and they have to face up to the fact that it was you who succumbed.

When you know you have got your priorities all mixed up, admit it. Say, "It wasn't Fleur's fault; I wanted to try that extra strong beer and I was stupid. I am sorry." It may not make your parents feel any happier about your friendship, but it will increase their respect for you and reassure them that you are adult enough to admit to being wrong.

If you find yourself faced with a stand off situation, try to negotiate. If your father forbids you to go out with your Jewish boyfriend because you are of different faiths, sit down and ask him just what it is that worries him. Suggest he takes the chance to get to know your boyfriend better and tries to judge him, not on his religious beliefs, but for his own sake. Do remember that, while your parents can say who does and does not enter their home, they cannot control whom you choose as a friend.

But also remember that when they seem to be interfering in your life, it is usually because they care so much that they want to protect you as much as they can.

THE FINAL WORD

This book contains no magic. Now that you have reached the final chapter, you won't suddenly discover that you are the world's best orator, or that you never feel tongue-tied or shy again. You will still have days when you ask yourself, "What am *I* doing here?" and others when you could kick yourself for saying something silly.

There will be times when you are tempted to curl up in a corner and hide rather than face the crowd and others when you feel you could take on the world. That's fine; it just means you're normal like the rest of us!

But you are also unique. There is no one else quite like you anywhere and your thoughts and feelings and ideas and aspirations are very important. So don't keep them all to yourself – get talking!

Other Piccadilly books by Rosie Rushton

You're My Best Friend – I Hate You
"Rosie Rushton runs through the joys and pitfalls of childhood friendship and gives lots of humorous but sensible advice on everything from how to be a good friend to how to live without one.
– Observer

Just Don't Make A Scene, Mum
This is the first title in the tremendously popular Leehampton trilogy about five teenagers and their very embarrassing parents.
"...cool and diverting comedy" – The Times

I Think I'll Just Curl Up And Die
They thought their parents couldn't get any more embarrassing – then they get worse!
"...juggles the humour, heartache and heavy-breathing with an easy balance of wit and sympathy" – Joanna Carey of the Guardian

How Could You Do This To Me, Mum?
Chelsea, Jemma, Sumitha, Jon and Laura are back again in another hilarious book!

Poppy
Poppy seems to have it all – she's pretty, popular, has a model family, and boys queuing up to take her out. So how will she cope when her secure environment crumbles around her?
Rosie Rushton writes with tremendous verve and empathy about some very nineties problems.

GLACIER BAY

NATIONAL PARK & PRESERVE

Above: Fairweather Range.

Front Cover: McBride Glacier, Muir Inlet.

Inside Front Cover-1: Dwarf fireweed blooms against a backdrop of the cloud-covered Chilkat Mountains.

Page 2: A solitary kayaker.

Back Cover: Bald eagle.

Editor: Angela Tripp
Art Director: Joanne Station
Writer: Darcy Ellington
Editorial Assistant: Karrie Hyatt

Albion Publishing Group
924 Anacapa Street, Suite 3A
Santa Barbara, CA 93101
(805) 963-6004
Lorie Bacon, Publisher

PHOTO CREDITS

Tom Bean: 11, 19, 21. **Carr Clifton:** Front cover, 4-5. **Jeff Gnass:** 8, 16, 20, 32. **John Hyde:** 10, 12, 13, 14-15, 29, 30-31, back cover. **Mark Kelley/Alaska Stock Images:** 2. **Keith J. Sutter:** Inside front cover-1, 6-7, 18, 22-23. **Tom Walker:** 24, 26, 27, 28.

ACKNOWLEDGMENTS

We would like to acknowledge and thank the following for their assistance and contribution to this book. The help of these individuals and groups has been invaluable: Marvin Jensen, Bruce Paige, Sharon Paige, and the staff at Glacier Bay National Park and Preserve; Leslie Sirstad and Melanie Nelson from the Annie Mae Lodge; Nena Berry; John and Betty Donohoe; Lewis Sharman; Greg Streveler; and Debbie Smith and everyone at the Alaska Natural History Association.

CONTENTS

GLACIER BAY National Park and Preserve is a place

filled with wonders. A place where great cliffs of ice tower above vast expanses of sparkling water. A place where rocky barrens devoid of life gradually give way to lush forests teeming with countless varieties of plants and animals. A place where the absolute stillness is broken by the booming thunder of a calving glacier. A

place where, as John Muir wrote nearly 100 years ago, "out of all the cold darkness and glacial crushing and grinding comes this warm, abounding beauty and life to teach us what we in our faithless ignorance and fear call destruction is creation finer and finer."

Creation is indeed the force behind the continually changing face of Glacier Bay. The park encompasses 3.3 million acres of pristine wilderness where change is the only constant. From the smallest lichen clinging to life atop a recently deglaciated boulder to the complex and unusually fertile marine environment thriving where freshwater meets the sea, the park is a living laboratory where the processes of geological and biological evolution are played out before our very eyes.

The variety of life in Glacier Bay is matched only by the diversity of the landscape. In a land where myriad images compete for attention against a backdrop of dense gray clouds, the spectacular is commonplace. Here, snow-covered mountain peaks soar above mist-

Face to face with the ice age.

shrouded inlets; deep, still waters rest utterly quiet and gray under a leaden winter sky; massive snouts of glacial ice move relentlessly down mountain valleys, transforming everything in their path; verdant forests come alive with bird song beneath a gently warming spring sun; and fantastically shaped icebergs, overwhelming in their stark beauty, dwarf even the largest of living creatures. This truly is a land of singular beauty—a land where discovery reveals the awesome perfection of nature's design.

Glacier Bay National Park and Preserve is located west of Juneau at the upper reaches of the Inside Passage. The park's namesake bay is a sixty-five-mile-long Y-shaped fiord where

the waterways and landscape are continually transformed by the advance and retreat of the many tidewater glaciers that converge here. About 600,000 acres of marine waters serve as both habitat for numerous species of fish and sea mammals and highway for the 150,000 people who visit the park each year.

Those who come to the park to experience the marvelous beauty of Glacier Bay firsthand are reminded that people are only guests here. The residents—bears, goats, moose, wolves, whales, and eagles to name just a few—call this land home.

This place is one of the few sanctuaries remaining in a world increasingly held hostage by people's needs and desires for food, timber, and ore. Because of its tremendous significance, Glacier Bay has been awarded World Heritage status by the United Nations. Citing the area's "outstanding universal value" to humankind, the UN designation will help protect the park in years to come.

Today, you are invited to take a closer look at the incredible amalgam of ice, rock, and water that is Glacier Bay National Park and Preserve. Prepare to be stunned by the spectacular sights and sounds, soothed by the timeless rhythms of nature, and humbled by the awesome forces that have shaped and continue to shape this dynamic land. It is an experience you will never forget.

WELCOME.

CHAPTER 1

A World Revealed

Magical is a word often used to describe Glacier Bay National Park and Preserve. From the Tlingit natives who have revered this place for countless generations to the explorers and scientists whose hearts and minds were captured by its beauty and mystery, Glacier Bay has always cast a powerful spell on those who have experienced its splendor.

A massive iceberg sculpted by the sun, wind, and rain.

Page 8: The vegetation in Lituya Bay is regrowing in the wake of a 1,700-foot tidal wave that swept into the area in 1958.

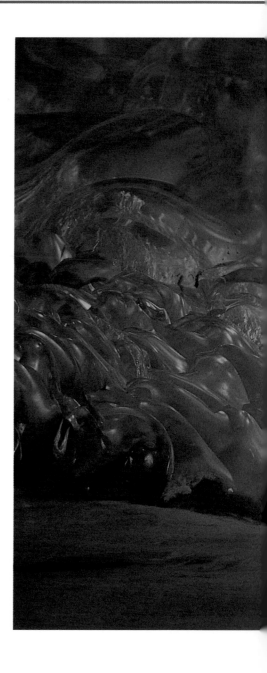

As in most of southeast Alaska, the land here in Glacier Bay is relatively young in geological terms. Many glacial advances and retreats have shaped and are continuing to shape the landscape of the park. Before the last great ice advance, which occurred 3,500 years ago, native Tlingits inhabited the region. They flourished in this rich environment by fishing from well-crafted canoes and hunting in the mature spruce and hemlock forests. The tales they left behind of their life in the bay continue to inspire their people even today. But when harsh climatic conditions brought about glacial expansion, the Tlingits were forced to abandon the area as the ice once again filled the bay. Although the Tlingits established a new community in nearby Hoonah, they never relinquished their strong ties to Glacier Bay.

They were destined, however, to lose their claim to the bay when the rest of the world discovered it. Recorded history for the region begins in 1741 when a Russian packet boat sailed into Icy Strait under the command of Alexis

Exploring an ice cave in the remnant of the retreating Muir Glacier.

Tchirikov. It was forty-five years before the next recorded landing was made on this wild coast by Captain James Cook, an English explorer.

Then, in 1786, French scientist and explorer, Jean Francois de Galaup, comte de La Perouse, anchored at what is now Lituya Bay. Unlike his predecessors, La Perouse spent nearly a month in the area and became well acquainted with the native people. He kept a careful account of his stay, including detailed descriptions of the natives and the surrounding wilderness.

Fifty miles south of Lituya Bay is Cross Sound. It was here in July 1794 that the HMS *Discovery*, under the command of Captain George Vancouver, was forced to drop anchor because of thick, floating ice. Vancouver dispatched two longboats to survey the area, and two days later his men sighted a five-mile-long bay. The bay ended abruptly in a massive wall of ice estimated to be 300 feet high and five miles wide. This was Glacier Bay. In the next 140 years, the glacial ice would recede about sixty miles, opening up a new land ripe for exploration.

Dundas Bay and the Fairweather Range.

Pages 14-15: Contemplating the scenery at Alsek Lake.

John Muir, the California naturalist, was the most famous of those to "discover" Glacier Bay. Muir, together with four Tlingit Indians and S. Hall Young, a Presbyterian minister, entered Glacier Bay by canoe in October 1879. Muir was thrilled by the chance to see the great ice giants at work molding the land and his enthusiasm for Glacier Bay proved to be contagious. His letters to a San Francisco newspaper attracted worldwide attention and soon resulted in the first tourists visiting the bay. Throughout the 1880s and 1890s, steamships made summer pilgrimages to the area.

Science, too, followed close on the heels of tourism. The Harriman Expedition, led by the famous railroad magnate Edward Harriman, made an important study of Glacier Bay. A gathering of scientists, artists, photographers, and writers—including John Muir—spent five days in the bay in June of 1899 taking pictures, making detailed observations, and collecting specimens. It was none too soon. That September, a devastating earthquake transformed the bay into an impenetrable maze of floating ice. For years the area remained inaccessible and this ended the tourist trade for a time.

In the decades that followed the earthquake, the ice in the bay continued to retreat at an astonishing rate—the fastest glacial retreat in recorded history. This phenomenon, with its inherent opportunities for study, along with the region's incredible beauty made Glacier Bay a natural candidate for federal protection. One man, an ecologist named William S. Cooper, made it his personal mission to see that Glacier Bay became established as a national monument, which it did in 1925 by President Calvin Coolidge's proclamation. A large addition was made to the park in 1978, and in 1980, Congress redesignated the area Glacier Bay National Park and Preserve.

Tlingit raven totem.

TLINGITS

Tlingit legends illustrate the deep connection the native people have with Glacier Bay. These oral traditions have no corresponding dates—unlike written historical accounts—but they demonstrate the long association between the native people and *Sit'Eeti Geey*, the bay from which the ice receded.

Prior to the last ice advance, Tlingit stories tell of a life of abundance lived in a valley through which flowed a river, called Chookan Héeni or Grass River. The inhabitants of this place were a maritime people skilled in both hunting and fishing. Several narratives reveal the Tlingit's pride in their ancient way of life and their historic ties to the bay. How then did they come to leave it? There are several versions of the story, passed on from generation to generation, which recount the desertion of the bay.

A young girl, known as Kaasteen, was kept in seclusion during her first menses. In her loneliness, she decided to call the glacier to her using a fish bone. In doing this, she inadvertently violated two taboos; not calling the spirits of the ice directly by name and not maintaining the self control expected of her during her training. Her mistake had disastrous consequences as the ice began to descend upon the village.

When the people saw what was happening, they realized that they would have to leave the bay. Kaasteen, because she had broken taboos by calling the glacier, wanted to stay behind. However, her grandmother, named Shaawatséek', spoke up, saying, "this granddaughter of mine is a young woman. Children will be born from her. So you will take her aboard with you. But whatever happens to my maternal uncle's house will happen to me."

The people tried to dissuade the old woman but she was determined to stay behind. They said good-bye to Shaawatséek' and sang of their grief as they left her and their land. Their songs are still sung today as part of very solemn occasions, especially in connection with the removal of grief.

CHAPTER 2

LAND IN MOTION

In terms of geological history, humankind's existence on earth can be char-acterized as lasting for the merest instant. Yet, our planet has been evolving for millions of years, and the forces that shape the land are so powerful and relentless that they are sometimes difficult to comprehend. In Glacier Bay, the forces of nature have conspired to create a place that is at once barren and life-giving—a place where the landscape is continually reborn.

Icebergs calving off Lamplugh Glacier.

Page 16: View across Lamplugh Glacier, Johns Hopkins Inlet.

Brady Ice Field.

The evolution of life here is profoundly affected by the same forces that shape the land. Changes wrought by wind and water affect the varied ecosystems, as does the powerful molding and shaping action of earthquakes and glaciers. Some of these events took place thousands of years ago and some are occurring today. The rapidity of change here makes it a natural setting for the study of geological and biological phenomena.

The extent of change in Glacier Bay can be measured by the tremendously varied topography of the park. The mountains are the dominant feature, uplifted by earthquakes and sculpted by earlier periods of glaciation. Several mountain ranges are encompassed by the park, including the southern Saint Elias, Alsek, Fairweather, Takhinsha, Chilkat, and Beartrack mountains. East of the majestic Fairweathers is Brady Ice Field, one of the largest ice fields in North America and the source of many of the massive glaciers in the park.

Scattered throughout the park and located primarily near the mountains are areas that appear to have escaped the ice for as long as 50,000 years. This type of landscape, called a refugia, is distinctive from recently deglaciated areas of the

park in that the geological features and vegetation are radically different.

Between the Fairweathers and the Gulf of Alaska is an eighty-five-mile-long strip of the park. There lies Lituya Bay, visibly altered by its history of giant tidal waves. To the north is the newest park addition, a 57,000-acre preserve along the lower Alsek River. This river, which merges with the Yukon Territory's Tatshenshini River, is one of the few river systems to transverse the coastal range from the subarctic interior. And everywhere there is ice and snow—a lot of it.

It is primarily the ice that is responsible for the incredible amount of change going on in Glacier Bay. The speedy retreat of the bay's glaciers provides observers with an up-close view of the processes that helped shape our world. During the last ice age, huge glaciers thousands of feet thick covered nearly all of Canada and the northern United States. Then, less than 20,000 years ago, the ice began to melt. The land revealed by the glaciers' retreat had been transformed by the relentless grip of the ice into a barren wasteland. Eventually, life returned to the denuded ground. Although this process ended in places like Chicago and Detroit thousands of years ago, it is still happening in Glacier Bay.

Cinquefoil and immature Sitka spruce.

Pages 22-23: The face of Lamplugh Glacier dominates the landscape.

A trip up the bay is like taking a journey back through time. At Bartlett Cove, where the land has been ice free for 200 years, there is lush spruce forest. At the upper reaches of the fiords where the ice has been only yesterday, there is naked rock. Throughout the expanse of the bay, one can bear witness to the process by which plants reclaim the land.

Plant recovery begins with algal growth, which stabilizes the silt and retains water. Soon tufts of moss are present. The moss is followed by scouring rush, fireweed, dryas, alder, and willow. Dryas and alder help fix the soil with nitrogen, which in turn enables spruce to take hold. Eventually, the spruce crowd out the alder but ultimately lose the battle to the hemlock, the next dominant tree in the forest. A mature forest represents the climax of this process.

Each type of plant that occupies an area creates conditions that change the environment. These changes lead to the plant community's replacement by other communities better suited to the new conditions. Over time, a succession of different plant communities occupies the environment, one after the other. Scientists believe that the study of plant species' interactions with each other and with their surroundings may produce information that could help us cope with natural and human-made environmental disasters. Glacier Bay does indeed provide an invaluable opportunity to learn and to understand—an understanding that may be crucial to our ongoing effort to define humankind's relationship with the natural world.

Margerie Glacier, Tarr Inlet.

GLACIERS

Although these giant masses of ice appear as immovable as any mountain, the truth is that they are anything but static. Glaciers are forever changing, engaged in an unending dance of advance and retreat. The only thing constant about glaciers is their ability to transform the landscape.

The story of a glacier's life begins high in the mountains where heavy snowfall exceeds snow melt. As the snow accumulates, it is compressed into granules of ice. Because it becomes increasingly heavy, the ice mass submits to gravity and begins to flow downhill, becoming a virtual river of ice. When a glacier gains ice and moves forward, it is said to be advancing. But if the loss of ice at the lower elevations is greater than the amount of snow amassed in the mountains, then the glacier's terminus, or end, begins to retreat.

When an advancing glacier's terminus overshoots the land and begins to move into the sea, it becomes a tidewater glacier—one of nature's most spectacular offerings.

Much of a tidewater glacier's activity depends on the depth of the water at its face, where the glacier and the sea meet, and on the amount of terminal moraine present there. If the terminus lies in shallow water, it is supported by a shelf of sediment and debris called a moraine, which is pushed out ahead of the glacier during its advance. A terminal moraine prevents ice from breaking off the glacier, a process known as calving. If the moraine is lost or diminished through glacial retreat or if the terminus advances into deeper water, then ice is calved at an accelerated pace.

Over a dozen tidewater glaciers averaging 150 feet high and over a mile wide converge in Glacier Bay. The calving of huge chunks of ice, which become icebergs in the bay, is a regular occurrence and contributes to the fast rate of retreat. The glaciers' extremely rapid retreat, which has been occurring for the past 200 years, has been the most studied in history.

CHAPTER 3

UNTAMED EXISTENCE

Wilderness, by definition, is both a wild, uncultivated region and a bewildering mass or collection. In the case of Glacier Bay, both happen to be true. In the park's 3.3 million acres of glacial barrens, alpine meadows, great forests, and sparkling waters lives an amazing variety of fish and wildlife. The park contains myriad ecosystems, from those just evolving to those that are quite old in comparison. The ecosystems sustain many habitats where a broad array of creatures have found their niches.

Steller sea lion.

Tufted puffins.

Page 24: A fast-swimming salmon is no match for a black bear.

Probably the most critical of these habitats, in terms of its relationship to the rest of the ecosystems, is the marine environment. The waters of Glacier Bay provide an exceptionally productive biome, or life zone, for microscopic plants such as phytoplankton, which are the basic element of the food chain on which all life depends. Each summer, these plants explode in a huge bloom that supports the abundant assortment of marine life found here.

Halibut, capelin, king salmon and dungeness crab—all are here. Orca whales, minke whales, harbor porpoises, and humpback whales also benefit from the fertile sea. Harbor seals select their meals from the ocean smorgasbord and then retire to the nearest iceberg to digest them.

Spawning season for the salmon draws birds and mammals to the banks of creeks where they engage in a feeding frenzy. Sockeye, chum, silver, and pink salmon all spawn in the park's streams. Dining on them are bald eagles, ravens, wolves, coyotes, otters, seals, minks, and both brown and black bears. Just how the salmon are able to find their way back to these streams where they were born—after years in the sea—is still a mystery.

More of the sea's riches are made available to shore dwellers via the sands of

the park's beaches. Barnacles, mussels, and sea urchins provide food for many animals, including coyotes and black bears. Brown bears, also known as grizzlies, have been observed digging for clams on the outer coast.

Birds are also found here in abundance. More than 200 species of birds have been sighted in the park. Many are seen near the water. Kittiwakes wheel and dive at the faces of tidewater glaciers. Large flocks of gulls, murrelets, and northern phalaropes gather at bay mouths and narrow waters where turbulence brings food closer to the surface and within easy reach of hungry beaks.

The diversity of the landscape contributes to the wide variety of species found here. Islands and cliffs attract nesting tufted and horned puffins, glaucous-winged gulls, and oystercatchers. Tidal flats and shallow waters are home to many kinds of waterfowl. Snow buntings feed on ice worms atop glacial barrens, and in the forests, the songs of thrushes, kinglets, and blue grouse are heard.

Spring and fall migrations also affect the bird populations within the park. Most species are more abundant in the summer months. Some, such as the arctic tern, journey as far as 20,000 miles round trip to hatch their young here. Others, such as the bald eagle, can be seen year round in most areas of the park.

Other types of animals are present in some parts of the park but not in others. Moose, common in Muir Inlet, are seen throughout Glacier Bay from time to time. Lynx and wolverines, scarcely glimpsed by people, keep to the backcountry but sometimes venture closer to the more visited areas of the park. Deer and beaver are also rarely seen but do appear occasionally in some areas.

One animal that lives throughout the park is the bear. Brown bears are common on the outer coast of the park and in the West Arm of Glacier Bay. They are rarely spotted elsewhere. Black bears, however, are found everywhere. The sharing of the park by bears and people can sometimes be problematic. Visitors are encouraged to learn about the bears' habits and to take steps to prevent surprise encounters. Aside from the danger they present to humans, bears themselves are endangered if they abandon traditional fishing grounds or other food-source areas to avoid people.

The peaceful coexistence of people and wildlife presents one of the major challenges facing the park today. The impact of both science and tourism are still being studied but some adverse effects are obvious. Careless visitors who approach wildlife too closely are responsible for many mishaps. Human beings are guests here, and as such are urged to respect their host, Mother Nature.

This is an extraordinary place. In a world increasingly altered by human encroachment, Glacier Bay has been set aside as a sanctuary. It belongs to all of us but it is held in trust for future generations—and we are responsible for its continued preservation.

Pages 30-31: A pod of humpback whales.

Below: Mountain goat.

A humpback whale breaching.

HUMPBACK WHALES

Where are the whales? is a query put to park employees every summer by visitors eager to catch a glimpse of these captivating creatures. Perhaps it is their kinship with humans that so fascinates us. Sixty to 100 million years ago, ancestors of the whales existed on land rather than in the ocean. These primitive species evolved into the air-breathing, warm-blooded sea mammals that we know today. Their huge size makes them seem like giants to us, yet they are defenseless against their greatest enemy—humankind. Now our interest is crucial to their survival.

One species of whale that is facing extinction is the whale visitors ask about when they visit Glacier Bay—*Megaptera novaeangliae*, commonly known as the humpback whale. *Megaptera*, meaning large winged, refers to the humpbacks' long pectoral fins; *novaeangliae* refers to New England where the first large populations of humpbacks were observed and described. Today, the migratory humpbacks are found in every ocean on the planet.

Although this universality might suggest abundance, the opposite is true. An estimated 150,000 humpback whales flourished in prewhaling times but today only 10,000 exist worldwide. Like other types of whales, humpbacks live in family groups, cooperate with each other to obtain food, and communicate with a variety of sounds. Yet, of all whales, humpbacks delight human observers like no other whale. Known as the gymnast of the sea, the humpback is able to execute amazing leaps and turns out of the water with its unique pectoral fins. This type of jump, known as breaching, is far more acrobatic than that of most whales.

The large tail fin, or fluke, is also used by the humpback in a practice known as lobtailing, or tail slapping, in which the whale stands on its head and repeatedly strikes the water. Although the humpback creates a lot of noise and huge splashes, scientists do not know the purpose of

this practice. Many speculate that it is perhaps a form of communication—even a warning of danger. Another form of communication that is more easily identifiable is the distinctive song of the humpback. While wintering in its tropical mating grounds, the humpback can be heard producing a sound that is unlike that of other whales. It is often the haunting voice of the humpback that most people associate with whale song.

Southeast Alaska's humpback population travels to Hawaii and Mexico to mate and give birth. During this period, the whale does not feed and therefore must store enough fat in summer to last the rest of the year. Since an adult humpback averages forty to fifty feet in length and weighs about three quarters of a ton per foot, this is no small feat. Humpbacks are baleen whales, so called because they filter their food through hard, comblike pairs of plates called baleen. The plates have bristles on the end, and, as the whale scoops large quantities of sea organisms into its mouth, the plates act as filters, which trap the food and release the water—about 150 gallons at a time.

Glacier Bay humpbacks feast on a diet of shrimp, various fish such as capelin, and krill, a tiny shrimplike organism. They have been observed working both alone and in groups to trap their food by casting a "net" of bubbles, expelling air underwater and using the bubbles to drive their prey together where they are more easily consumed.

The opportunity to see a humpback feeding, breaching, or merely gliding gracefully through the water in Glacier Bay is an increasingly rare privilege. Humpback populations in the bay may have declined somewhat in recent years. Whether this is due to a natural cycle or occurs in response to human activities is not known. Nevertheless, humpback whale behavior is being intently studied in an effort to save these extraordinary creatures.